Effective Classroom Learning

Effective Classroom Learning

A Behavioural Interactionist Approach to Teaching

Kevin Wheldall and Ted Glynn

BASIL BLACKWELL

British Library Cataloguing in Publication Data

Wheldall, Kevin, *1949–*
    Effective classroom learning: a behavioural
    interactionist approach to teaching. — (Theory
    and practice of education)
    1. Schools. Teaching. Applications of
    behavioural sciences
    I. Title II. Glynn, Ted III. Series
    371.1'02

    ISBN 0-631-16825-7
    ISBN 0-631-16826-5 pbk

Library of Congress Cataloging in Publication Data

Wheldall, Kevin.
    Effective classroom learning: a behavioural interactionist approach to teaching/
    Kevin Wheldall and Ted Glynn.
        p.   cm.
    Bibliography: p.
    Includes index.
    ISBN 0–631–16825–7 — ISBN 0–631–16826–5 (pbk.)
    1. Teaching. 2. Learning. 3. Child psychology. 4. Classroom
management. I. Glynn, T. (Ted) II. Title.
    LB1027.W47 1989   88–34294
    371.1'02—dc19   CIP

Typeset in Sabon 10 on 11½ pt
by Photo·graphics, Honiton, Devon
Printed in Great Britain by
Billing & Sons Ltd, Worcester

Contents

For Susan and Vin

Editor's Preface

Very few, if any, educational problems are straightforward enough to have simple answers. Therefore, in so complex a human activity as educating, it should be no surprise that yet another series can still have a vital and significant contribution to make to our understanding of educational problems. Theorists and practitioners in the many developing interests in education quite properly continue to want to share their views and findings with others.

Theory and Practice in Education attempts to present, in a readable form, a range of issues which need to be considered by serving and student teachers in their roles as practitioners. Wherever formal, organized learning exists in our schools and colleges, there will always be questions relating, for example, to the effectiveness of teaching and children's learning, the preparation and adequacy of what is taught, the processes of assessment and evaluation, the sensitive problems of accountability, the preparation of children for 'life' and the monitoring of innovations.

Behaviour modification, or applied behavioural analysis, as it is now called, has been and doubtless always will be one of the major techniques of classroom practice. Teachers, whether they realize it or not, employ the behavioural approach in most aspects of their work with pupils. Yet surprisingly when confronted with this suggestion, some teachers either refuse to accept it or on accepting it have no inclination to examine and apply the principles systematically. But most teachers are keen to learn more about the underlying effects of their actions and to channel these to good effect.

Kevin Wheldall and Ted Glynn have become international figures in this field and the series is lucky to bring them together in this book. Their concerns are essentially practical and classroom orientated. In *Effective Classroom Learning*, they present a case for a behavioural approach to teaching, covering both classroom management and instruction. Most recent thinking in behaviourism has turned attention to 'behavioural interaction'. This aspect, which uses all the characteristic methods of applied behavioural analysis, is carefully defined in the text and it promises to herald a new and stimulating dimension to classroom learning and teaching.

Behavioural methods are most frequently associated with special education. It is important to emphasize that this book is much broader and will be found valuable by teachers anywhere in the system.

University of Leeds *Dennis Child*

Foreword

This book attempts to provide a contemporary 'behavioural interactionist' perspective on teaching. It is based on the programmes of behavioural research in schools we have both been engaged in, sharing the aim of trying to make classroom learning more effective and more rewarding for both teachers and pupils. Although our two research centres are separated by some 13,000 miles, for 10 years we have enjoyed a fruitful and collaborative research relationship. Reciprocal visits, a reasonably efficient postal service and the wonders of modern information technology have permitted us to share ideas readily and to organize complementary research in a number of important areas.

For some time we had daydreamed about the possibility of integrating our research findings into a book. This has now been made possible by the generous support of the British Council who, recognizing the value of the work produced in our two research centres, have provided funding for an academic-exchange scheme. This has allowed reciprocal visits by the authors (resulting in this book) and has also permitted exchange visits by our doctoral students working with us in the area of behavioural research in schools. This book would not have been possible without support from the British Council and we would like to take this opportunity of recording our grateful thanks.

Although our names are on the cover, the research and ideas reported in this book are by no means all our own. We have both been fortunate in having research colleagues and doctoral students who have made creative and original contributions to the programmes of research we have been privileged to lead. The following have all made major contributions to the research and theory reported in this book: Keith Ballard, Susan Colmar, Diane Dolley, Vin Glynn, Wilson Henderson, Steve Houghton, Stuart McNaughton, Frank Merrett, Mariane Quinn and Viviane Robinson. We would like to thank them all for their inspiration and friendship over the years. There have also been many other undergraduate and graduate students, too numerous to mention, who have researched with us and whose work has helped to build up the profile of research reported here. Finally, we would like to thank Frank Merrett (again) for producing the very professional index.

Kevin Wheldall and Ted Glynn

1

Why Can't Schools be More Positive?

Imagine how you might feel if you found yourself sentenced to a term of periodic custodial care for over ten years. Forced to spend up to six or seven hours a day locked up with 20 or 30 others, you are subjected to a regime of petty discipline, of performing mindless, repetitive tasks which have no meaning, and of continual criticism of your appearance, your behaviour and your attitude. In the struggle for survival among so many others, and at the mercy of fickle custodians whose moods and motives are hard to fathom, you find your sensitivities becoming brutalized. Any respect you had for those above you diminishes daily as you encounter apparently arbitrary timetabling, changes of task and changes of staff. Told that this is for your own good, to equip you for later life outside in 'the real world', you laugh hollowly and long for the day of your release . . . . when you can leave school.

This might sound like a wicked travesty of schooling to many teachers, but too many children in our schools feel this way. They are put off education by the trappings of schooling. Even with the phasing out of corporal punishment, days spent in school can be demoralizing, demeaning and soul-destroying. In recent years, some educationists have begun to doubt the value of much of what currently passes for schooling. John Holt (1969), for example, has written movingly of the fear that schools can hold for many children. Many educationists are beginning to ask if schooling and education have very much in common or are even compatible.

The strange thing is that we take schools for granted. We tend to see schools as being an obvious, necessary and permanent part of our own lives when we are children and of our children's lives when we grow up. Schools are places where we are expected to send children for over ten years so that they can be taught the academic and social skills necessary for survival in adult life. After all, how else would they learn? But only a moment's reflection reminds us that it was not always so. Schooling for all children as a matter of course is a relatively recent innovation. In some developing countries, even today, there is not such a heavy reliance on formal schooling. But we take it as given that schooling is essential for effective education. Furthermore, we give tacit acceptance to the view that schools have to be like they are. In this book, we will argue not that schools are unnecessary, but that they are not always as truly educative as we would like them to be. Schools can be alienating, aversive and unresponsive. We would like to see schools become more positive, more liberating and more effective.

Courses of training for teaching universally lay great stress on knowledge of curriculum design and content, on the philosophical, historical, sociological and psychological perspectives on education, and on the in-depth study of one's main academic subject. Relatively little time, however, is spent on preparing the teacher-to-be in the interactive skills essential for successful classroom teaching. Very little instruction is provided in what the teacher actually ought to do in the classroom, how she or he should behave. This is particularly noticeable in the context of handling troublesome or disruptive classroom behaviour. Many student teachers are still reassured with the pious platitude that provided you have spent enough time preparing your lessons properly, you will never have discipline problems. The poverty of this advice is exposed by the countless number of both student and practising teachers who have had lessons which were impeccably prepared destroyed beyond redemption. Many have been reduced to tears by classes of children whose behaviour in the classroom was beyond the influence of any amount of prior lesson-preparation.

Teaching practice can be a curious business. Student teachers are sometimes left alone for large periods of time to cope, as best they can, with whole classes of children, with little or no guidance as to how to proceed once they are actually in the classroom. The lucky ones may receive useful (or otherwise) tips from more experienced staff. The type of advice commonly offered is 'Give them hell for the first week, assert control, take charge, show them who's boss, and then you can relax.' Others rapidly acquire the skills of sarcasm and 'put down', learned from colleagues (who should really know better) or perhaps dimly remembered from their own school days. Many wish that an effective model of teaching was available which offered practical advice about how one should actually behave in the classroom. We believe that our *behavioural interactionist* approach to teaching, the unifying theme of this book, will go a long way towards fulfilling that wish. In essence, this approach requires that teachers behave in a more positive and more responsive way towards children and that classrooms and schools are structured to become more meaningful and more effective learning contexts.

SCHOOLS CAN BE AVERSIVE

But many schools still seem to operate on the principle of punishing unwanted behaviours irrespective of whether those behaviours reflect failures to learn or anti-social acts. Even today school rules all too frequently consist of a list of 'Thou shalt not's. (We heard of one school rule which said baldly: 'No banging of anything on anything'!) Appropriate behaviour is demanded rather than encouraged or taught, and examples of appropriate behaviour are rarely specified. Children are hardly ever involved in the process of making the rules which describe behaviours appropriate and acceptable in different learning contexts.

About ten years ago one of our students analysed the results of a small, fairly informal survey he had conducted in a large urban comprehensive school in the UK. Nearly three-quarters of the fifth-year boys reported being both hurtfully hit by teachers and officially caned (of these over 65 per cent felt it was deserved). Only half of this proportion of second-year boys had been officially caned but just as large a proportion had been hurtfully hit. Figures were generally much lower for girls.

Holt (1969) writes of 'why intelligent children act unintelligently at school.' The simple answer, he claims, is 'because they're scared . . . . most children in school are scared most of the time, many of them very scared.' Children are scared, not only of physical punishment, which has at long last been abolished in British state schools, but also of being verbally abused, sarcastically scored off, shown up in front of peers and generally demeaned. Many children may also be frightened that behaviour appropriate to their cultural, ethnic or home settings will be judged out of place or inadequate in the classroom and school setting. This is conducive to learning neither academic skills, nor appropriate social behaviours, nor tolerance and acceptance of people who are different.

There is also an ethical dilemma in allowing children to remain in a context over which they have little control and where they have no alternative behaviours to those being punished. This can arise when children display embarrassed giggles or resort to funny remarks in situations when they cannot answer the teacher's question, or find the teacher's question has little meaning to them, or find the task set too difficult. Punishing children in such circumstances is particularly reprehensible since they can neither comply nor escape. When teachers repeatedly punish children in these circumstances, it is hardly surprising that the teacher may rapidly become someone to be feared and avoided. There are even some teachers who deliberately seek this status for themselves as a means of establishing control. For such teachers almost all learning difficulties are seen as issues of control. They could not be more wrong.

As an illustration, take the following example. When writing this chapter in a crowded library, one of us was disturbed by two students talking in loud stage whispers. After a while, he glared across at them and their irritating behaviour ceased. However, within a few minutes the whispering had started up again. The author's power to 'control' the students' behaviour was brief and limited. Punished behaviour is merely temporarily suppressed and is likely to recur once the punishment or fear of punishment is removed. Consequently, one needs to continue punishing to suppress a behaviour over a period of time. To do this effectively one needs tighter and tighter control over the students and over their opportunities to escape. This has a number of implications. First, the mere fact of repeating the punishment is likely to lessen its effectiveness. Second, this may precipitate the escalation to more severe punishments. Third, children may become adapted to tolerating high levels of punishment. Fourth, and most important, nothing of educational worth has been achieved by such an interaction.

But why do teachers continue to resort to punishment since it is ineffective and has so many drawbacks? One possibility is that they continue to punish because occasionally this has led to the immediate (but temporary) stopping of an unwanted behaviour. In so far as teachers find this rewarding (they get a brief respite) they will continue to punish children. Teacher behaviour has come under the control of the reward obtained from the brief respite. The teacher and children are thus literally locked in a vicious circle. This is hardly a positive context for learning.

A moment's thought reveals the nonsense of attempting to teach by means of punishment. Consider a simple learning situation where a teacher, Mrs Sharpe, wants a young child, Mervyn, to get on with his work and not to chatter, not to look out of the window, not to get out of his seat, and not to disturb other children. So, she decides to punish Mervyn by reprimanding him whenever he does anything other than get on with his work. Mervyn bumps his neighbour; she reproves him. He gets up; she reproves him again. He looks out of the window; she reproves him again, louder this time. He begins to wail and she smacks him. Mervyn wails louder than ever. The teacher feels exhausted and miserable. She has tried to solve this problem in terms of exerting total control over Mervyn's behaviour, ending with physical force. But her exhaustion and misery tell her that she does not have this control over Mervyn. All of her attention has been focused on only one child. She has ignored the other 29, who are now all watching her and Mervyn, and still she has not succeeded in teaching him to get on with his work. All of this points to the simple fact that it is far more constructive to focus on appropriate behaviour than it is to try to suppress the inappropriate behaviours.

Delivering punishment has another danger: it paves the way for teaching other undesirable and unhelpful behaviours. By definition, we do not like or 'go for' punishment; we attempt to avoid it. Consequently, we rapidly learn ways to do so. This may sometimes include doing what the teacher had in mind, but may more frequently include escape behaviours such as opting out of the teacher's area of control whenever possible, or trying to undermine that control. As Becker, Thomas and Carnine (1969) remark; 'Avoidance and escape behaviour often have names such as lying, hiding, truancy, cheating in exams, doing things behind one's back, etc. Accompanying such avoidance and escape behaviours are negative feelings for the persons who use punishment. . . . . the teacher is wise to find other means for influencing children.' Avoiding the teacher, running out of the class, 'skipping' class or staying away from school are behaviours which will be rapidly learned. These behaviours constitute an escape from punishment. It seems reasonable to suggest that truancy, school phobia or school refusal may often be simply the product of a school environment which the child finds either aversive or lacking in positive interactions compared with what is available outside. We would argue that in order to be successful, schools must be places where appropriate behaviour is negotiated and rewarded. The main emphasis should be on creating positive, responsive learning contexts which will not only make teaching more effective and efficient, but will also make school a more enjoyable and happy environment for both children and teachers.

It is only fair to emphasize that corporal punishment has finally been abolished in British state schools. The results from schools which abandoned these barbaric and inefficient methods are encouraging. The number of physical attacks on teachers by pupils dropped dramatically following the decision to outlaw corporal punishment in inner-London schools. In Scotland it was shown that schools which had abolished corporal punishment did not suffer a decline in discipline and that none of these schools wanted to reintroduce corporal punishment. As this evidence accumulated it became increasingly hard to justify Britain's place as the only European country which continued to beat its children in school. It is to be hoped that countries like New Zealand will also formally abolish corporal punishment in the near future.

SCHOOLS CAN BE OFFENSIVE

Schools can also be alarmingly rude places. Pupils are continually reprimanded for bad manners or insolence, but the example set by some teachers is unlikely to lead to better behaviour. The man or woman in the street will often claim to be able to tell when a new acquaintance is a teacher. Is it something about the edge in their voices or do some aspects of their behaviour at school carry over to life outside?

Imagine going to a social event with, say, 20 or 30 other people only to find that you had a very strange host. . . .

'Oi! Bryant!', he shouts in an imperious voice and snaps his fingers as he says the one word 'Window!'

Chris Bryant, looking rather sheepish, reluctantly opens the window.

Jean Simpson, a timid soul, half raises her hand and asks tentatively, 'Do you think I might put my jacket back on?'

'No, weakling, do as you are told! You'll only go to sleep if you get too warm,' sneers our host and turns to catch a couple arriving late, trying to sneak in through the back door unnoticed.

'Ah, Swan and Peacock, not very early birds are we? Too busy, were we, to arrive at the same time as everyone else, ... liaising with the P.M. perhaps . . . .' His sarcasm falters in mid-flow as he spots another guest.

'Melrose, what are you wearing? You look like a hibernating hamster! We wear blue pullovers, don't we? Get outside and change it and do something about that stupid haircut while you're at it. I don't trust people with fringes. . . .'

What a host! It could only be Basil Fawlty or an insensitive teacher with his class. For where else could anyone get away with this sort of rude behaviour other than in a school? From almost no one but a teacher (or a sergeant-major) would we tolerate such personal remarks and insulting comments. Fortunately, all teachers are not as extreme as the one we have satirized above but we have met teachers like this and so, we suspect, have you. Clearly there are times when children are expected to cope in very unnatural learning contexts; contexts which are not predicated upon mutual respect and understanding between tutor and learner, but which instead emphasize authority relationships and control, often in a rude or aversive way, and which focus on the trivial at the expense of the important.

It seems to us that schools can often be very unnatural places for effective learning to take place. In addition to the aversive and abusive aspects in some teacher–learner interactions emphasized above, there are also the problems associated with sheer size. Large groups of learners are commonly herded together into relatively small rooms with, typically, only one teacher available to meet their learning needs. Many teachers interpret this context as one of control rather than interaction. In this book we will repeatedly refer to the need for responsive one-to-one contexts for learning certain academic skills. But with such numbers and such teacher–child ratios, this might, at first, sound like crying for the moon. We will discuss, however, the important role of parents and peers as resources available to all teachers and schools. Education means much more than mere schooling, and we should be trying to devolve more power and responsibility back to the family and community from which it was previously appropriated. Parents and peers have important teaching roles to play in the education of children.

Class size also creates other problems. Few of us would find it too difficult to engage two or three children in productive learning. Families manage it with ease most of the time, especially if the children vary in age and the older ones can help in taking care of the younger children. But engaging a class of 30 children, all of the same age, in worthwhile learning activities is a different matter. In these circumstances teachers are forced to employ rather different strategies. Not all such strategies are conducive to effective learning, and they are by no means always positive in orientation. In this book we will also show how effective classroom management of children's social behaviour can be achieved in positive ways. Again this depends upon developing more responsive social contexts so that effective learning can take place.

We believe that, in spite of the many disadvantages that are inherent in schooling, all teachers can learn to make schools more positive and hence more truly educative environments. To this end, we will outline our approach to education which we call a behavioural interactionist perspective. We will present our basic model and show how it can be applied in schools to create more effective learning contexts for children. But first we need to review the origins and development of this approach.

2

A Behavioural Interactionist Perspective

Some children present a major problem to teachers. They may appear to be 'developmentally delayed', 'ill-prepared for school', or even 'operating under a totally different value-system'. These are only other ways of saying that they behave differently from so-called 'normal' children. They may not talk much or, perhaps worse, they may appear to listen less; they may refuse to pay attention; they may well not find schoolwork rewarding; they may indulge in anti-social behaviours; they may swear or fight. In fact they may not do many of the things you expect children to do and yet they may do many things you do not want them to do! Difficulties such as these can best be understood in terms of the child's previous learning experiences and the child's current learning environment. Knowledge of how such learning takes place and how to make it more effective is of obvious concern and interest to any teacher.

The principles underlying contemporary behavioural psychology have direct practical applications in the classroom. However, not all such applications are equally useful. By employing a behavioural approach to teaching, effective classroom management (rather than control) can be achieved in a positive, non-punitive way. But, of course, teaching involves much more than this. Although management of children's social behaviour in the classroom may well be a necessary condition for effective academic learning to take place, it is not a sufficient condition. Even the most well-ordered classroom will fail to bring about good academic progress in its learners if insufficient attention is paid to the process of academic instruction. A behavioural approach has an important role to play here too, as we will demonstrate. Our concern will not be so much with curriculum content: that is primarily the professional responsibility of the teacher. But we will indicate how children can best be helped to learn important academic skills through the use of tried and tested behavioural approaches to teaching. We will discuss how responsive social contexts for effective teaching can best be structured. We call our approach a 'behavioural interactionist' perspective to distinguish it from other behaviourally derived approaches to teaching which, in our view, are unnecessarily restricted and restrictive in their effects on both teachers and children.

But what is a 'behavioural interactionist' perspective, and what characterizes a behavioural approach? Before attempting to discuss what we can achieve in the classroom, we need first to review general behavioural principles and how they evolved from the school of psychology known as behaviourism.

A BRIEF HISTORICAL SURVEY

Pavlov's Classical Conditioning

The roots of behaviourism may be said to lie in the work of the Russian physiologist I. P. Pavlov on what came to be known as classical conditioning. Since Pavlov's work is so well known ('Pavlov, that rings a bell!'), and since its applications to classroom teaching are few, we will mention it only briefly here. It is important to emphasize, however, that Pavlov's work had a profound influence on both J. B. Watson, the 'founding father of behaviourism' and B. F. Skinner, the researcher who took up Watson's mantle to produce 'radical behaviourism', accepted by many as providing the most adequate descriptions so far of the basic operating principles of human behaviour. However, Pavlovian conditioning procedures are also important in their own right to an understanding of some aspects of human behaviour, especially emotional behaviour. They are applied clinically, for example, in behaviour therapy for treating obsessive fears.

Watson's 'Behaviourist Manifesto'

The unchallenged father of behaviourism was J. B. Watson, who pioneered this dramatically different approach to human psychology in the United States at the beginning of this century. After working with animals and developing methods for studying animal psychology, he became convinced that such methods were not only equally applicable to the study of human psychology, but that they were also the only scientifically reputable way of doing so. Watson's behaviourism was based largely on Pavlovian classical conditioning. In 1913 he published what became known as the 'Behaviourist Manifesto' in which he stated the case for a new human psychology based on objectivity and the importance of learning. Brushing aside introspection of inner mental life, he demanded that psychology concentrate purely on what could be observed, i.e. behaviour. He insisted that concepts be both carefully defined and experimentally demonstrable. Both Freudian and instinctual theories of human behaviour were rejected on these grounds; they were vague and virtually untestable. Alternative explanations, many highly speculative, were offered by Watson, based primarily on extrapolations from Pavlov's work on conditioned reflexes. He attempted to explain even the most complex aspects of human personality by 'millions of conditionings' of basic reflexes.

Watson was personally so convinced of the importance of learning –at the expense of hypothesized, but unproven, beliefs that behaviours are innate – that he sometimes made outrageous statements such as:

> Give me a dozen healthy infants, well formed, and my own specified world to bring them up in and I'll guarantee to take any one at random and train him to become any type of specialist I might select – doctor, lawyer, artist, merchant-chief, and, yes, even beggar-man and thief, regardless of his talents, penchants, tendencies, abilities, vocation and race of his ancestors. (1913).

> The behaviourists believe that there is nothing from within to develop. If you start with a healthy body, the right number of fingers and toes and eyes, and the few elementary movements that are present at birth, you do not need anything else in the way of raw material to make a man, be that man a genius, a cultured gentleman, a rowdy or a thug. (1928)

This was, clearly, naive and extreme environmentalism – the belief that human behaviour is totally learned from the environment in which the person is reared – as opposed to nativism – the belief that a person's potential is biogically fixed at birth. No applied behaviourist would argue so extreme an environmentalist view today, since it has been convincingly demonstrated that heredity exerts a powerful influence on an individual's achievements. In fact, even Watson admitted that he was exaggerating when he made his claims and B. F. Skinner has subsequently said, 'I have never known any behaviourist, with one exception, who has denied the very considerable role of genetic endowment' (Cohen, 1977). As Huxley (1964) has powerfully declared, extreme environmentalists (such as Watson) 'forget that even the capacity to learn, to learn at all, to learn only at a definite stage of development, to learn one thing rather than another, to learn more or less quickly, must have some genetic basis'.

Acknowledging the role of heredity and genetic endowment, however, does not necessarily mean accepting that, for example, 'intelligence' (a very controversial concept) is inherited – what is inherited may be something much more basic, such as susceptibility to different forms of conditioning. Nor is accepting the role of heredity to deny for one moment the essential plasticity of human behaviour, which allows considerable and continual remoulding by the environment. So-called 'low' or 'poor' intelligence in a child, which may in part be (in some unknown way) genetic in origin, may possibly prevent the Watsons of today turning out 'doctors or lawyers', but this restriction is only at the upper end of complex skilled behaviours and still allows extensive scope for changing the child's behaviour. Children with severe intellectual and physical disabilities are capable of meaningful learning in an appropriately structured educational context. In fact, it is probably true to say that few children are prevented from achieving their goals by genetic limitations since children's performance is so rarely maximized by environments designed to optimise appropriate learning. Furthermore, applied behavioural learning theory has allowed genetically and otherwise biologically damaged children with severe intellectual disabilities to achieve levels of skill far in excess of anything that would previously have been expected from children labelled and rejected as 'untrainable vegetative retardates' and hence, in the past, excluded from education.

Skinner's Operant Conditioning

The work of B. F. Skinner is frequently misunderstood and even more frequently misrepresented. Many otherwise well educated people dismiss his ideas without clearly understanding what they are. They often confuse them with classical conditioning and believe that he is a strong advocate of the use of punishment. As Skinner himself once said in an interview 'It's quite surprising how little the world in general knows about operant conditioning, and that world includes many psychologists.'

Skinner's theory of learning was initially formulated as a result of his research with rats and pigeons. Basically, he argued that any responses emitted will increase in frequency if they are 'reinforced'. For example, when children follow the teacher's instruction they may be reinforced by teacher praise. Similarly, when teachers respond to the ideas children express they may reinforce the production of those ideas by their manifest interest and comments. Reinforcers are very difficult to define. In the strict technical sense they refer to any things or events which when following a certain behaviour lead to an increase in the frequency or probability of that behaviour. (This is known as an operational definition.) But basically reinforcers are things that individuals will seek out:

> Good things are positive reinforcers. The food that tastes good reinforces us when we taste it. Things that feel good reinforce us when we feel them. Things that look good reinforce us when we look at them. When we say colloquially that we 'go for' such things, we identify a kind of behaviour which is frequently reinforced by them. (Skinner, 1971)

Hence, food will reinforce a 'hungry' (food deprived) individual; sexual gratification and the alleviation of thirst may also act as reinforcers. These reinforcers are examples of unconditioned positive reinforcers. Because they appear to be innate, they may be said to be unconditioned (or unlearned), and because we usually seek them out, they may be said to be positive.

Aversive consequences are things and events that we seek to avoid. Avoiding them is itself reinforcing and this process is known as negative reinforcement. An example of a negative reinforcer is a teacher who stops nagging once his pupils have complied with his demands. Children will learn to engage in behaviour which will stop the teacher nagging. Hence their behaviour may be reinforced negatively as well as positively.

Punishment is quite different from negative reinforcement. Punishment consists of presenting the aversive consequence in an attempt to reduce the frequency of behaviour. For example, the teacher gives a child detention for arriving late at school. Skinner considers punishment to be an unreliable and time-consuming way of preventing behaviour from occurring and does not give it much emphasis in his writings. We should note that removing positive reinforcers is also a form of punishment. Teachers sometimes 'fine' pupils for misbehaviour by deducting points from their team, for example. This is known as response cost.

Some teachers react adversely when they hear that a behavioural approach to teaching has its origins in work with rats and pigeons. They protest that it demeans us to attempt to reduce our behaviour to the level of animal behaviour. But few would deny the benefits of medical advances initially pioneered with simpler animals. Similarly, it makes sense that behavioural procedures were initially pioneered with animals, where there is less (potential) risk and where greater precision can be achieved within experiments. Of course, these findings would not necessarily be directly applicable in the study of human behaviour and none of what we have said is meant to suggest that we are, or should be, trying to apply the same procedures directly with children in schools. Nor need we concern ourselves in this book with studies carried out with animals, since there is now a wealth of material reporting research with human subjects. Countless demonstration studies of effective behavioural procedures have now been reported, carried out in natural settings such as hospitals, classrooms and homes. More importantly, recent applied research has been designed specifically to address questions arising from current good teaching practice. This research focuses on behavioural interactions between learners and teachers and on the balance of power between them rather than simply on what one needs to do to control the behaviour of the other.

Baer, Wolf and Risley's Applied Behaviour Analysis

Over 20 years ago three psychologists in the United States were concerned at the slowness of psychology in applying to human learning and development the behavioural principles pioneered by Skinner and his associates. These three psychologists, Don Baer, Montrose Wolf and Todd Risley, turned their concern into action. They pooled their efforts and resources and began a major and systematic research programme from the Department of Human Development and Family Life at the University of Kansas.

Together with their many colleagues, they developed and refined techniques for objectively observing and recording child and adult behaviour in everyday contexts. They pioneered the application of powerful research strategies to allow objective evaluation of a variety of procedures for changing behaviour in parenting, in childcare and in primary, secondary and tertiary educational contexts. These strategies and procedures effectively defined a totally new perspective and field of study, known as Applied Behaviour Analysis.

In their seminal article, Baer, Wolf and Risley (1968) outlined the distinguishing characteristics of this new field. To qualify as applied behaviour analysis, research had to meet a number of carefully specified criteria.

First, the *applied* criterion required that researchers should address a real problem which had real social significance. For example, children's high rates of disruptive behaviour in the classroom have serious implications both for their own educational achievement and for their teachers' skills in managing the classroom.

Second, the *behavioural* criterion required that the problem had to be solved and the variations in child and adult behaviours had to be spelled out in sufficient concrete detail so that other reseachers reading a research report could correctly identify and measure the same specific problem behaviours.

Third, the *technological* criterion required that any behaviour-change procedures employed also needed to be spelled out objectively, so that other researchers or readers of the research report could replicate the same specific procedures or strategies. Techniques for behaviour change had to be presented in terms of observable objective behaviours to be performed by a parent, teacher, peer or researcher.

Fourth, the *analytic* criterion required that research needed to employ a stringent research design, which could demonstrate convincingly a) that the procedure was effective and b) that the observed effect could be clearly attributed to the specific procedure used. The field of applied behaviour analysis made a major methodological contribution to educational research by introducing strategies which allowed the analysis of behaviour within classroom and school learning contexts. This was achieved by precise, repeated measurement of the behaviour of individual children and adults. This was an important advance over the prevailing large-scale descriptive-correlational approaches to studying human behaviour employed in educational research. These correlational studies did not easily identify definite causes of children's learning difficulties and so were of little help in suggesting appropriate solutions.

Fifth, there was the criterion that applied behavioural research should be *conceptually systematic*. This meant that concepts and measures developed in a variety of different settings could be brought together within one coherent framework. In this way, research in settings as different as pre-school or childcare centres, rest homes for the elderly and school playgrounds, employed common definitions and common measures, such as 'engagement with available objects and activities', 'on-task behaviour' and 'staff attention contingent on on-task behaviour'. This has resulted in better understanding of staff behaviour, of staff training and of the day to day operation of 'living environments'. The behaviour of staff in all these different environments has been found to have a number of important features in common, for example a low rate of staff attention for children or adults who are behaving appropriately. Hence, data from one context have contributed to the development of training programmes in other contexts. In other words, what has been learned in one setting has contributed to the development of programmes in other settings.

Since 1968, the *Journal of Applied Behaviour Analysis* has disseminated high quality behavioural research across a wide variety of educational settings, addressing numerous important social and educational questions. Twenty years of systematic research in families, homes, communities, schools and institutions has dramatically increased our understanding of behavioural principles and how to apply them successfully in the real world. All of this work owes an enormous debt to B. F. Skinner who has lived to see the applications of his earlier scientific work throughout society.

There are many other aspects of behavioural research and theory which we have not yet described but it is preferable to move on to the classroom setting and to introduce any further new concepts, as necessary, in their teaching context. We are now in a position to review the lessons learned from our brief historical overview and to clarify exactly what we understand by a behavioural approach to teaching.

THE FIVE BASIC PRINCIPLES OF A BEHAVIOURAL APPROACH TO TEACHING

A behavioural approach to teaching offers a theoretical basis for understanding much of what is happening in classrooms. More importantly, it has an accompanying methodology for approaching and analysing problems and a technology for solving them. As we hope to show, a behavioural approach offers positive alternatives for improving both classroom management and academic learning. We believe that a behavioural approach to teaching, if implemented with sufficient skill, will yield both more effective teaching and a more rewarding teaching experience. A behavioural approach to teaching is based on several general assumptions which Wheldall and Merrett (1984, 1987a) have summarized as five general principles of 'positive teaching'.

1 *Teaching is concerned with the observable* A behavioural approach to teaching is objective and is concerned with observable behaviour. Teachers who adopt a behavioural approach concern themselves with what children actually do, i.e. their behaviour, rather than speculating about unconscious motives or the processes underlying their behaviour. For example, a teacher might report that 'Sally worked well for the first half of the lesson but then her concentration lapsed.' In behavioural terms what happened was that Sally completed ten maths problems correctly in the first 20 minutes of the lesson, but only two in the last 20 minutes. The teacher's reference to her concentration lapse is an attempt at explanation based purely on speculation. Similarly, to say that Sarah is 'hyperactive' *because* she is often out of her seat does not get us any further and is unhelpful. This is an example of what are known as 'explanatory fictions'. They do not explain anything but merely restate the problem in different words. But in the process these speculations can be turned into convenient labels, which are sometimes used as an excuse for doing nothing about the problem behaviour. We will return to this point later.

If we accept that the only way that we can really know what an individual can or will do is through observing their behaviour (including their verbal behaviour) then it follows that careful definition and observation of behaviour will be central to a behavioural approach. Being concerned with observable behaviour, however, does not mean that children's and teachers' beliefs and feelings are to be ignored. Rather, these can be understood best in the context of the observable behaviours which accompany them.

2 *Almost all classroom behaviour is learned* The sorts of child behaviour that teachers are likely to be concerned with are almost all learned as a result of interactions with home, classroom and school environments. This does not mean that we fail to recognize the importance of genetic inheritance, as we have already made clear, nor does it mean that we believe that anybody can be taught to do anything given time. Rather, we believe that genetic or biological endowment may set limits to what an individual can learn, but that behaviour is still the result of learning interactions. We take the practical view that while there is very little we can do about children's genetic inheritance or the biological state of their nervous systems, we can provide them with contexts which make it easier for them to learn. Central to a behavioural approach is the view that intellectual and social skills as well as inappropriate or unacceptable behaviours

are all learned. Children can be helped to learn new skills and more appropriate behaviours.

3   *Learning involves change in behaviour*   The only way that we know (that we can know) that learning has taken place is by observing changes in behaviour. Teachers should not be satisfied with claims such as 'I think Mark has a better attitude towards school now.' We need evidence that Mark now behaves differently, by coming to school regularly perhaps, or by handing in his homework on time. This concern with changes in observable behaviour as evidence for learning is critical to a behavioural approach, as we shall see in the following chapter.

4   *Behaviour changes as a result of its consequences*   Individuals (children and teachers) learn on the basis of tending to repeat behaviours which are followed by consequences which they find desirable or rewarding. They tend not to repeat behaviours which are followed by consequences which they find aversive or punishing. In other words, the consequences of behaviour are critical for learning. A behavioural approach to teaching emphasizes positive consequences (or positive reinforcement). This implies that teachers will need to examine and change their own behaviour if they seek to change children's behaviour. They will need to learn how to use positive reinforcement to the best effect. In the following chapter we will discuss in some detail the need to use reinforcement selectively. We are *not* advocating an approach based exclusively on providing extrinsic positive consequences for every classroom learning situation. This can be educationally limiting and can interfere with the power of naturally occurring reinforcers available in educational contexts. We will focus on the careful use of the least intrusive reinforcers necessary to do the job. Often these are naturally occurring reinforcers. We will also emphasize 'contingencies in context': the importance of the settings in which behaviours occur and are reinforced. This brings us to the final principle.

5   *Altering the context can change behaviour*   In any situation some behaviours are more appropriate than others, and we learn which situations are appropriate for which behaviour. If a child's behaviour is appropriate for the circumstances in which it occurs it is more likely to be rewarded; if it occurs in inappropriate circumstances, reward is less likely; and behaviour which might be appropriate in one context may even lead to punishing in another context. As a

result of this we rapidly learn not only how to perform a certain behaviour, but also when and where to perform it. Some early behavioural programmes controlled the learning context so tightly that they may have unintentionally caused children to limit their performance to that one narrow training context.

Similarly, some situations make certain behaviours more possible. You cannot play football without a ball being available. The presence of attractive books makes reading more likely in the same way as a positively disposed interacting adult makes child language more likely. On the negative side, crowded conditions will make pushing and shoving more likely to be a problem. This all points to the need for teachers to think carefully about the settings or contexts they wittingly or unwittingly have contrived in their classrooms. Again, we will consider this in more detail in the following chapter.

The five points set out above are essential features of any fundamentally behavioural approach to teaching. Such an approach tries to demonstrate functional relationships between behaviours learned and factors in the environment, i.e. what environmental factors are likely to lead to what forms or rates of behaviour. As we have already said, this approach assumes that almost all of the behaviour with which we are likely to be concerned as teachers is learned, and that it is learned and maintained by environmental influences. The direct application of this to teaching lies in the fact that if we can change environmental contexts or consequences then we can change children's behaviour.

A BEHAVIOURAL INTERACTIONIST PERSPECTIVE

There is an unfortunate, but widely held, misconception about those who advocate behavioural approaches to education. Some teachers assume that behaviourally oriented educationists are necessarily unquestioning supporters of the educational status quo wedded to the simple task of making schools more efficient, critical of sloppy classroom-teaching methods yet never questioning the underlying values of or the necessity for schooling. But not all those who espouse behavioural methods are conservative adherents to educational orthodoxy. Some of us even regard aspects of contemporary classroom practice as incompatible with education. It is perfectly consistent with a *contemporary* behavioural approach to share with others the view that schools can be alien and artificial learning environments which bear only a passing resemblance to learning situations in the world outside the classroom. This may be true especially for those children marginalized by their social background, culture, ethnicity, gender or disability. We believe that the inappropriate and ineffective learning contexts in which these children find themselves can be made more appropriate and productive by the skilful use of contemporary behavioural methods. More effective and more responsive educational contexts and strategies can be developed, which are also more likely to result in academic behaviours and skills being learned, maintained and generalized.

Behavioural approaches to teaching have long offered powerful technologies for bringing about dramatic changes in classroom behaviour. There is little doubt that behavioural methods can be used to reduce disruptive and off-task behaviours and to increase appropriate social behaviour and the work output of pupils. Questions that ethical educationists then have to ask themselves are: How far are we justified in doing this? Are we not in danger of using our behavioural knowledge and skills to support an educational system about which we have doubts? By helping teachers to develop more positive and more effective classroom management skills, are we propping up ineffective and unresponsive teachers?

One does not have to be a Marxist to view disruptive pupil behaviour, sometimes, as a legitimate reaction to uninspired teaching, unreasonable demands and dull lessons, and to contexts in which learners have little or no control over their learning. However, there is little doubt that for successful teaching to take place, effective classroom management is essential. Classroom management of children's social behaviours in order to increase the amount of time children spend academically engaged in relevant learning-tasks is a necessary (but not sufficient) condition for academic progress. To put it more simply, well-prepared curriculum materials may have little effect if the children are unable to attend, or are prevented from attending, because of disruptive behaviour. More positive teaching methods, as we shall see, will help to establish a classroom context in which disruption is minimized and academic engaged time is maximized, allowing effective learning to take place. One important component among these methods is assisting teachers to share some of their control over learning interactions.

But a behavioural approach has far more to offer teaching and learning than just effective classroom management. It will also help us to identify ways of teaching which encourage the learning of relevant academic skills in classroom settings, and ways of facilitating the generalization of these skills to the world outside the classroom.

In the past, some behavioural psychologists believed that skills and bodies of knowledge could, and should, be broken down into a series of so-called behavioural objectives which when appropriately sequenced and taught to mastery level would guarantee effective learning. The idea was that the steps would be so small that errorless learning would be possible. This ignores the fact that errors, properly responded to, can be very powerful learning opportunities. More recently, however, behavioural psychologists have turned to analyses of existing effective learning strategies which occur in the world outside the classroom, with the aim of identifying effective natural teaching strategies.

In British educational psychology the enthusiastic application of behavioural objectives to curriculum design has led to the neglect of the child's behaviour as exerting an influence on the teacher's behaviour. Such a curriculum becomes both 'teacher-proof' and 'child-proof', an achievement which some psychologists seemed to be proud of! Living, interacting human beings become an irritating intrusion into a perfect system. The system and the curriculum are then in danger of becoming fixed, being seen as the only way to learn, the only path for all children to follow. But we know that learning in the world outside the classroom is not like this. Individuals learn similar skills and concepts and master similar areas of knowledge by very different routes and processes. There is no one yellow brick road to success. Our own behavioural approach seeks to take account of this and to optimize natural learning situations, not construct artificial ones. If we are genuinely concerned about aims of autonomy and independence in learning, then we need to discover and analyse those characteristics of educational environments which support and promote *independent* learning.

Schools often function in such a way that responsive social contexts, where interactive learning can take place, seldom occur. Children may have minimal opportunity to initiate interactions or to share a task with an adult or another more competent person. Programming, timetabling and school routines may provide few opportunities for children to initiate. Teachers may be so engaged in presenting instruction to children or in classroom routines that they cannot, or do not, respond interactively when children do initiate. As we shall see, some of our recent research has shown, for example, that in British infant classes about three children, on average, may be waiting for teacher's attention at any one time, and this number increases as the lesson goes on.

In this book we will draw on our own recent research to show that responsive social contexts which allow learners to initiate as well as to respond, which provide shared tasks that promote reciprocal gains in skill between teacher and learner, and which provide responsive rather than corrective feedback are particularly powerful contexts for independent learning. Some of the current classroom and school contexts in which children learn, however, may be counter-productive, in that they may be reinforcing excessively dependent learning-strategies. We will return to this important issue in chapter 7.

The form of educational context we envisage from our behavioural perspective is very different from the commonly held view of what a 'behaviourist' classroom must be like (a 'clockwork curriculum'). We are also totally at odds with those who would seek to devise a programmed behavioural curriculum, built on tightly specified behavioural objectives and 'quality-controlled' by endless behavioural check-lists. In some respects, our perspective represents an attempt to implement child-centred learning within a behavioural framework.

We are now in a position to put together the various ideas we have introduced so far into a conceptual framework: our 'behavioural interactionist perspective' (Wheldall and Glynn, 1988). It is behavioural, since it builds on the methods and principles of behavioural psychology. It is also interactionist, since it is based on the central idea that we all learn from each other by interacting with each other. Our behavioural interactionist perspective is characterized by the following ten points. It is a perspective which:

1 *Employs the methods of applied behaviour analysis*   In both research and practice, we have a commitment to employing behavioural methods. We emphasize systematic, repeated measurement of observable behaviour and we make use of the logic and strategies of behavioural research. We will discuss this in more detail in the following chapter.

2 *Recognises the importance of natural settings and contexts*   We pay particular attention to the relevant settings and contexts which occur in the natural environment and how they will influence children's learning. More effective strategies for bringing about improved learning are likely to be developed if we take settings and contexts into account.

3 *Strives to maximise the use of naturally occurring reinforcers*   We attempt to employ naturally occurring reinforcers whenever possible as positive consequences for behaviour since they are more

likely to ensure the generalization of the learned behaviour to the wider environment. Artificial contingencies of reinforcement need to be employed selectively if they are not to prove counter-productive.

4 *Responds to evidence from non-behavioural research* We do not assume that only those who adopt a behavioural approach have something worthwhile to offer. Contemporary developmental psychology, for example, is a source of valuable information about adult–child interactions in natural settings. Findings based on research carried out from other theoretical perspectives can inform and improve our models of academic skills-learning and teaching.

5 *Emphasises the interactive nature of learning* We avoid one-way explanations of learning and embrace an interactionist perspective which recognizes that teacher or tutor behaviour will and should change in response to learner behaviour as well as learner behaviour changing in response to teacher or tutor behaviour.

6 *Seeks to assist children to assume a greater degree of control over their own learning* In order to help children become independent in learning, we should provide them with learning contexts which allow them to take a greater degree of control over their own learning. Consequently children should be allowed more choice of topic, timing and context of learning interactions. So-called 'child-proof' materials are alien to this approach.

7 *Focuses on broader educational issues than just schooling* We recognize the limitations imposed by some formal schooling practices and we attempt to redress them by providing children with opportunities to learn relevant academic and social skills in naturalistic contexts. We do not assume that effective answers to educational questions necessarily lie with schools or with teachers alone. Both parents and peers can be highly skilled tutors of academic skills and can afford a great deal more time in one-to-one interaction with children. Their contributions to children's learning has been greatly under-valued and under-used.

8 *Encourages initiations by the learner* We aim to provide contexts which promote initiations by the learner and which encourage teachers to respond to those initiations. This aim is shared with those who advocate child-centred approaches to learning.

9 *Values the learning opportunities provided by errors* Errors provide useful learning opportunities. They inform both learners and teachers about strategies needed to overcome learning difficulties. Behavioural methods designed to promote errorless learning deny learners and teachers access to these opportunities.

10 *Recognizes the complex professional skills required of teachers* We firmly reject the idea of attempting to produce 'teacher-proof' instructional materials, which degrade the professional role of teachers. Behavioural research should be attempting to equip teachers with a range of skills and procedures which have been shown to be of direct practical use in constructing appropriate learning contexts for children in their care. These include modelling appropriate academic and social behaviour, and sharing skills with and working in partnership with parents, peers and para-professionals in the use of behavioural procedures to enhance children's learning.

These, then, are the ten characteristics of our behavioural interactionist perspective. (This perspective is discussed more fully in Wheldall and Glynn, 1988.) As we have already said, we have felt it important to spell out clearly the sort of behavioural approach we are applying. We would not want our behavioural approach, which focuses on the interactive nature of human learning to be confused with other, more programmed behavioural approaches to teaching and learning. Our concern is with using contemporary applied behaviour analysis to help teachers develop responsive social contexts for children so that effective learning can take place. In the following chapter we will discuss in more detail the three essential elements of behaviour analysis: antecedents, behaviour and consequences.

3

The ABC of Teaching

Some of the common features of a behavioural approach to teaching include the need for gathering objective and systematic information, the need for continuous measurement and the need for instructional decision making to be data-based (as well as child-based). Teachers employing such behavioural procedures may be characterized as being responsive to data. They change or modify their teaching behaviour in response to objective information about their own and their children's performance. In this book we will introduce various ways in which teachers may change their behaviour in response to information about their own behaviour as well as that of their pupils.

A behavioural interactionist perspective is clearly different from other behavioural approaches to education. But, in common with other behavioural approaches, it is based on what is known as the three term analysis of behaviour or the ABC model.

A   refers to the antecedent conditions, i.e. the context in which a behaviour occurs and/or what is happening in that environment prior to a behaviour occurring.

B   refers to the behaviour itself, i.e. what a child and/or teacher is actually doing in terms of observable events.

C   refers to the consequences of the behaviour, i.e. what happens after the behaviour has occurred.

The relationships between A, B and C – the antecedent conditions, the behaviour and the consequences – are known as contingencies. Behaviour analysis seeks to demonstrate functional relationships between behaviour and environmental factors (consequences and/or antecedents). Put more simply, this means that in a behavioural approach to teaching we seek to identify aspects of the teaching environment (either antecedents or consequences) which we can change to improve children's learning. We look out for changes we can make to antecedent events or to consequences which will encourage behaviours that are conducive to learning academic, intellectual and social skills. Let us examine the three factors in turn, starting with antecedents.

ANTECEDENTS

It is not sufficient to attempt to explain learning simply in terms of behaviours and reinforcers. Antecedent events also influence the occurrence of behaviour.

Antecedents can serve to prompt certain behaviours. Take the example of when a teacher leaves the room and the class is left alone. For some classes this occurrence may have become a cue for noisy, disruptive behaviour since there is no one around to reprimand the children. (Some classes even post a look-out to give a warning of when the teacher is returning!) When the teacher does return, the noisy disruptive behaviour will cease. We can see here that this specific antecedent condition influences this particular behaviour. This influence derives from its association with certain consequences. It also indicates that control over the learning resided almost entirely with the teacher.

Let us take another example. The teacher asks Jenny a question in class (antecedent event), the child gives a silly answer (the behaviour), and her classmates laugh (the consequence). Since this laughter is rewarding, we may expect Jenny to produce silly answers upon subsequent similar occasions. She will be less likely to do so, however, when her classmates are not there. The presence of classroom peers has been learned as a cue for her inappropriate misbehaviour. This example underlines the need to consider the context in which behaviours occur and how some antecedents develop their power to influence behaviour.

To take a third example, most teachers will have noticed how the behaviour of a class varies depending on who is teaching them or even depending on where they are being taught. In other words, children's behaviour comes under what behavioural psychologists call stimulus control, whereby different stimulus conditions prompt different forms of behaviour. Being in Softy Simpson's class may become the stimulus for unruly behaviour, for example, while few would dare even to breathe loudly in Biffer Barnes' class. Similarly, academic lessons held by necessity in the art and craft room may result in more disruptive behaviour than when held in a regular classroom. Being in the art and craft room has become associated with a different form of behaviour, involving more movement around the room perhaps and more interactions with others about one's work.

Within the classroom environment a wide range of antecedent events will influence behaviour. They influence behaviour in at least two ways. First, there are those antecedent conditions which provide direct constraints or opportunities for behaviour. We are thinking here of factors such as seating arrangements, the presence or absence of particular materials or curriculum aids or the availability of an interacting adult. Second there are antecedent conditions which have acquired power over certain behaviours by association with rewarding or punishing circumstances, as we showed in the examples above.

The heading of antecedents encompasses a variety of features of the environment which may potentially influence behaviour. These range from specific events such as questions, directions or instructions to more enduring aspects of the environment. We have proposed a convenient division of these more enduring antecedent events into ecological factors and setting events (Wheldall and Glynn, 1988). By ecological factors we mean the more global aspects of the classroom environment such as heating level, lighting, arrangement of furniture and materials and classroom seating arrangements. In chapter 5, we will discuss in some detail the powerful influence of seating arrangements on both children's and teachers' behaviour. By setting events we mean social, contextual factors which can alter the characteristics of social interactions by their influence on the behaviour of individuals. Setting events, then, refer to more social features of the environment usually, but not always, involving the behaviour of others. Examples would include teacher-modelling of behaviours, the presence of an interacting responsive adult, a group activity and peer-tutoring situations. The concept of the setting event was first discussed by Bijou and Baer (1978) and later extended by Wahler and Fox (1981). Because setting events strongly influence the quality of teacher–child interaction that can take place, knowledge of their operation is vital to a behavioural approach to classroom teaching.

This key behavioural principle, that children's behaviour can be greatly influenced by antecedent contextual factors (whether ecological factors or setting events) appears to be little appreciated and greatly under-utilized in classroom teaching. Certainly, earlier behavioural approaches to teaching appear to have ignored the fact that learning can be facilitated or inhibited by altering antecedent conditions or settings within the classroom as well as by using procedures based on reinforcement. This is not to deny the importance or power of positive reinforcement from teachers; but we believe that good teaching requires that reinforcement procedures should be used more selectively and discriminatingly, as we will emphasize in the following sections.

The work of Risley (1977; Krantz and Risley, 1977) in the United States and our own work in New Zealand and the UK (Glynn, 1982 and 1983; Wheldall, 1981 and 1982) has sought to demonstrate the power of antecedent control of behaviour in classroom settings. We have attempted to show that by employing procedures based on changes in ecological factors or setting events we can often influence behaviour simply and successfully. For example, one of our research students (Frewin) completed a study in New Zealand which clearly demonstrated that the presence of an adult near the jigsaw table in a daycare centre greatly increased the number of children participating in that activity, even though that adult was not directing or instructing children to do jigsaws. Similarly, we found that the playground participation of 11–12 year olds increased, and inappropriate behaviour decreased, when participating adults were introduced into the school playground than when additional equipment was provided (O'Rourke and Glynn, 1978). Participating adults were a more powerful setting event for a high rate of playground participation by children than the additional equipment. Along with these increased rates of engagement in playground activities there were decreases in disruptive and aggressive behaviours. In the course of this book we will provide many other examples of the power of both setting events and ecological factors as influences on children's behaviour in school.

Setting events such as the presence of a responsive adult, sequencing of lesson activities, provision of appropriate or inappropriate curriculum material, and clear and consistent use of instructions have all been found to influence children's behaviour in classrooms, as have ecological factors such as seating arrangements and the location of classroom furniture. Teachers employing a behavioural approach will strive to identify which particular ecological factors and setting events in their classroom have clear effects on children's learning. When teachers make effective use of antecedent events to encourage appropriate behaviour, there is less need for frequent interruptions to the lesson to praise or reprimand children's behaviour. Teachers will also have more time to spend on teaching and instruction, particularly on one-to-one interactions.

BEHAVIOUR

What do we mean when we talk about the concept of behaviour? And why do we place such great emphasis on specifying exactly what behaviour a child is displaying? These questions are fundamental to a behavioural interactionist approach to teaching. As we said in the previous chapter, increasing use of objective behavioural observation arose as a reaction to the highly speculative approach of early psychologists who attempted to 'explain' human behaviour by recourse to inborn 'instincts' and to irrational, uncontrollable, unconscious forces. Watson rejected such notions and demanded that psychology should be based on the observable. Consequently, the tradition began for careful, objective recording of children's behaviour and the contexts in which that behaviour occurs. Children's behaviour refers to what children actually do, and we attempt to describe this in as precise a way as possible. If we observe Susan building a tower with bricks, we would not write down just 'creative play' since another observer or someone else reading our notes might interpret 'creative play' differently. It is too vague and imprecise. We would record that she stacked four bricks. This is likely to be more useful in conveying information about Susan's progress. However, if we were genuinely interested in Susan's creative behaviour, we might also record events other than just stacking four bricks. Susan might surprise us all with her initiative. She might arrange the bricks in a novel fashion.

Similarly, if Mrs Archer tells us that Jason is 'always messing about' in class, we need to ask her to define the behaviour more clearly. What she regards as 'messing about' may not be what we regard as 'messing about'. Moreover, if Mrs Archer uses a vague definition there is no guarantee that it is the same sort of behaviour she is categorizing in this way two days running. So we would ask her to list any of Jason's behaviours which she finds objectionable and then to define them as precisely as possible. A behaviour which is frequently found at the top of many teachers' lists is 'talking out of turn'. If we define this as 'any talking by a child when the teacher has requested the class to get on with set work quietly', then we are moving closer to an objective definition. The more objective our definition, the easier it is for two people to agree that a certain behaviour has occurred and the easier it is to count instances of such behaviour. However, we should be wary of specifying or operationalizing our goals or objectives so narrowly that we lose much of their meaning. For example, there is more to being engaged in a class lesson than the specification that children should be seated on their chairs.

Nevertheless, precise definition of behaviour also helps us to avoid the opposite danger of over-interpretation and giving non-explanations as causes of behaviour. Non-explanations sometimes take the form of what we referred to earlier as 'explanatory fictions' (Vargas, 1977). These are generally unhelpful while providing a veneer or gloss of 'scientific' explanation. They can also be dangerous in so far as they can be used to label children. Labelling a child is often coupled with the assumption that little can be done about improving his or her difficulties: the problem is seen as located within the child and not in the behavioural interactions. For example, if Darren keeps hitting other children his teacher may describe him as being an aggressive child, but if we ask her how she knows this, she may reply 'He keeps hitting other children.' The word 'aggressive' has become simply a label for a child who frequently hits other children but is sometimes used as if it were an explanation or cause of this behaviour. A further difficulty with such labelling is that it characterizes only one aspect of a child's behaviour. For example, Darren might also display some highly appropriate or co-operative behaviours.

Observing Behaviour

A behavioural interactionist approach to teaching implies that we will define objectively the types of behaviour we wish to encourage and measure children's progress by observing and recording changes in those behaviours. Once we have defined the behaviours objectively, we observe children and record the frequency with which those behaviours occur.

The behaviours we opt to observe will vary enormously and the way they are recorded will vary too. We might count the number of times Martin gets out of his seat in an hour; how frequently Rebecca asks for help every day; the number of words Terence speaks to his teacher; the amount of time class 4B spend getting on with their work; the number of words Janet writes in her daily diary; the number of maths examples Tony completes each lesson. Some behaviours record themselves (words written, books read, artwork produced) while others we have to observe and record (out of seat, shouting out, asking questions, initiating interactions).

Let us say that we are concerned about Jeremy who is not taking much part in class discussions; in fact, he hardly ever makes a contribution. To ensure that our impression or understanding of the problem is correct, and as a basis for later comparison, we need to collect baseline data. In other words, before we do anything about changing his behaviour we try to obtain an accurate picture of his current behaviour. Indeed, we have an ethical obligation to do this. Since we appreciate that class discussion is an important part of children's education, we include a regular 15-minute 'news' slot at the start of each school day, as well as encouraging class discussion at other times by responding to children's initiations. Children signal that they want to contribute by putting up their hands. So we count the number of times Jeremy puts up his hand to offer a contribution during the 15-minute period. We might also record the behaviour of two or three other children too, in order to see if Jeremy's contribution is much different from that of others in the class. We would not normally be satisfied with just one sample of behaviour from only one session. Jeremy may have had an 'off' day, as we all do from time to time. We want a sample which reflects his usual pattern of behaviour and so might observe him every day for a week, or even two weeks. After five days we see that his signalling to offer a contribution was as follows: day 1–0; day 2–1; day 3–0; day 4–0; day 5–1. His behaviour is clearly and regularly at a very low level in contrast with the other children we observed who are all volunteering contributions three or four times every lesson.

It is outside the scope of this book to detail the many and varied ways in which behaviour can be observed. Readers are referred to *Positive Teaching* (Wheldall and Merrett, 1984) for an introduction to this area. Complex observation schedules are not always necessary. Observations can be recorded on very simple record forms. These are simply convenient ways of recording observations in a systematic way for ease of transcription and scoring. The most simple procedure is probably to tally the occurrence of each behaviour you are observing within each observation session. In our research, however, we have often been interested both in how much of the lesson observed children in the class have spent working, and in the nature and frequency of teachers' responses to their behaviour. For this purpose we developed a schedule known as OPTIC (Observing Pupils and Teachers In Classrooms). OPTIC allows the observer to sample systematically positive and negative teacher responses to children's academic and social behaviours and also children's on-task behaviour. Studies carried out by our students working in pairs have shown the schedule to be both reliable and valid. A full account of OPTIC and its development is to be found in Merrett and Wheldall (1986). We will refer to it on subsequent occasions in this book when reporting research studies.

Behavioural Research Designs

Once having collected observational data over several sessions, it is important to examine these data for patterns or trends. In order to do this we construct a simple graph which is known as the baseline. Referring back to our earlier example of Jeremy's contributions to class 'news' times, we would draw a graph to show the number of volunteered contributions per session. The results we cited earlier are straightforward, but what if the results had been 0; 2; 4; 6; 8; or even 5; 4; 3; 2; 1 ? In the first case we would have evidence for an ascending baseline, i.e. the behaviour is improving without any help from us. In the second case, we would have evidence for a descending baseline which shows that Jeremy is contributing less and less often, under the present classroom conditions.

If we have an ascending baseline for behaviour which it is desirable to increase, it is difficult to know if anything we do will have any effect, since the frequency of the behaviour is increasing anyway. If we had only observed on the first occasion we could have been seriously misled. This is why we try to observe behaviour long enough to be able to see whether there is a clear trend in our graph. We usually continue to observe until we see a stable baseline, a fairly steady line on our graph. If the behaviour we aim to increase shows a descending baseline, but starts to go up following our introducing some change, then we are able to tell that our action is having some effect. Sometimes we get an uneven, 'lumpy' baseline when we plot our observations on a graph. The behaviour goes up one day and down the next. This is usually an indication that there are already powerful factors influencing the child's behaviour which should be looked into. For example, if we noticed that the number of words Malcolm writes in his diary goes up markedly every Tuesday and Thursday, we may find that this is related to his attendance at a local youth club on Monday and Wednesday evenings after which he has plenty to write about.

Ideally, and especially from a research point of view, a stable baseline is established before we intervene and alter some aspect of the environment (antecedent or consequence). When we intervene we continue to observe the behaviour and look for an appreciable increase in its occurrence as evidence for the effectiveness of our intervention. The graph of behaviour over repeated sessions provides us with a visual record of progress. Again, from a research point of view, we like to be able to demonstrate unequivocally that our intervention is the reason for the change observed in the child's behaviour. To this end, we employ two basic research designs.

The first is known as an ABA or reversal design. This design simply requires you to stop the intervention after a time and return to baseline conditions again. If it was your intervention that increased the desired behaviour, then taking it away should lead to a noticeable decrease in the behaviour. For example, you observe that Sam and Jimmy, who sit together, each write ten words on average per lesson during the baseline phase (A), and then you intervene and separate them (phase B). The graph shows that both boys now produce 30 words per lesson on average. To be sure that it is separating the boys that has had the effect on their behaviour, you now seat them back together again (phase A again), reverting to baseline conditions. You observe that the boys now produce around ten words each on average and conclude that you now understand at least one of the factors influencing their writing. You might then choose to separate the boys again and observe their writing increase a second time. This would then change the research design from ABA to an ABAB design.

The other main type of design is known as a multiple baseline design and there are three basic forms. The most common form is where you try out your intervention on a number of children but begin with each child at staggered intervals. For example, you begin observing Katy, Jenny and Gerald every day for 15 minutes during 'silent' reading, recording the amount of time they actually spend reading, or at least in visual contact with, their books. After a week, you give Katy a new natural language text to read; the other two carry on reading the books from the class reading scheme. You continue observing for a further week and then give Jenny a copy of the new book. After a further week, Gerald is also given one of the new books. If your graphs clearly show an increase in the amount of time spent reading for each child, following the change to the natural language text and not before, then you have good evidence for the effectiveness of your new books in increasing reading behaviour. This design is known as multiple baseline across subjects (which could be individual children or whole classes).

The second type of multiple baseline design involves a similar strategy but is concerned with just one child. In this case intervention is applied to several different behaviours which this child may have, but again is introduced at staggered intervals. This is known as multiple baseline across behaviours but we will not discuss it further since we will not be referring to it in this book.

The third type of multiple baseline design involves the same strategy and is known as multiple baseline across settings. In this design, an intervention is applied to the same behaviours in the same child or children but in several different contexts or settings. This type of design might be used to assess whether a new oral language programme will be effective for a given child when introduced into classroom, playground and home settings. We have briefly summarized these basic types of research design here since we will be describing research using some of these designs later in this book. For an extended treatment of this topic, see Barlow and Hersen (1984).

CONSEQUENCES

The final component in the three-term analysis of behaviour is consequences. As we said earlier, this refers to the fact that we tend to engage in behaviours which bring us what we want and to refrain from engaging in behaviours leading to consequences which we want to avoid. We all find food rewarding when we are hungry and we all find money rewarding; most of us also find praise and approval rewarding. And some of us find collecting train numbers rewarding. Thankfully, few of us find taking drugs like heroin rewarding. Within a behavioural approach to teaching, a major concern is to identify naturally occurring objects and events which children find rewarding and to structure the learning context so as to make access to these rewards dependent upon behaviour which the teachers want to encourage.

Negative Approaches to Behaviour Management

Consequences, as we have said, may be described as 'rewarding' or 'punishing'. Rewarding consequences, which we call positive reinforcers, are events which we seek out or 'go for', while we try to avoid punishing consequences; neutral consequences are events which affect us neither way. Behaviours followed by positive reinforcers are likely to increase in frequency. Behaviours followed by punishers usually decrease in frequency while neutral consequences have no effect. In a behavioural approach to teaching, infrequent but desirable behaviours (for example, getting on with the set work quietly) may be increased by arranging for positive reinforcers, such as teacher attention and approval, to follow their occurrence.

Undesired behaviours may be decreased by ensuring that positive reinforcers do not follow their occurrence. Occasionally, some teachers will find it necessary to follow undesired behaviours with punishers (for example, a quiet reprimand to an individual) in an attempt to reduce quickly the frequency of behaviour. But, contrary to popular belief, punishment plays only a very minimal role in a behavioural approach to teaching. One important reason for this is that punishment is antithetical to the maintenance of an educational context based on shared control between teachers and learners. Another reason is that what a teacher may believe to be punishing could, in fact, become reinforcing to the child. A child who receives little positive attention from adults may learn to behave in ways which result in adult disapproval. This child may prefer disapproval to being ignored and will continue to behave like this because any adult attention is positively reinforcing. This is commonly known as attention-seeking behaviour.

We have already noted that terminating a punishing consequence is also reinforcing and often serves to increase desired behaviours. This process is known as negative reinforcement. Again there are problems associated with its use since the child may rapidly learn other more effective ways of avoiding the negative consequence than the one the teacher had in mind. For example, a teacher may continually use sarcasm and ridicule with his pupils. He ceases only when they comply with his instructions. Another way for pupils to avoid this unpleasant consequence, however, other than by doing as the teacher wishes, is to stay away from school or to skip a lesson.

Punishment can also involve removing or terminating positive consequences (for example, by taking away a child's privileges). This form of punishment is known as response cost, and again there are problems associated with its use. From the teacher's point of view, it focuses on detecting non-compliant and inappropriate behaviour in preference to a more positive orientation which focuses on appropriate behaviour. From the child's point of view, response cost has the undesirable effect of reducing motivation since the child may lose, for example, privileges or points already earned for appropriate behaviour.

There is a misconception which confuses negative reinforcement and punishment. This is alarmingly common, especially in the writings of those criticizing behavioural approaches in education. There is no problem, however, if one remembers that the word 'reinforce' means to increase behaviour; a negative reinforcer increases behaviour when it is removed. We have frequently come across phrases such as 'negative reinforcement, that is, some kind of punishment, may be effective in extinguishing a response in a child.' Such a confusion has serious consequences and amounts to a travesty of what Skinner advocated. Skinner specifically argues against punishment as an effective means of controlling behaviours. He also emphasizes and deplores the pervasive use of negative reinforcement in maintaining many behaviours in everyday life. He argues that most people go to work not because they are positively reinforced by the job or the pay, but in order to avoid getting the sack or starving. He has consistently argued for harnessing the power of positive reinforcement to produce a better world (Skinner, 1948 and 1971).

Employing Reinforcement Constructively

'When he behaves as we want him to behave, we simply create a situation he likes, or remove one he doesn't like. As a result the probability that he will behave that way again goes up, which is what we want.' (Skinner, 1948)

What could be simpler? It sounds like common sense. But if it is common sense and we know all about reinforcement, why do children not behave as teachers and parents would like them to? The main reason is that parents and teachers, while sometimes claiming to use reinforcement, often do so inconsistently. It is commonplace to see people using methods of reward (and punishment) quite unsystematically and then wondering what went wrong.

Sometimes it is difficult to convince teachers and parents of the damage they do by being inconsistent. An example is the behaviour we call 'showing off' in young children; grandparents can be the arch-villains here. Not only do grandparents sometimes shower children with edible reinforcers (sweets, cakes, fizzy drinks) and praise, but they are also inconsistent. Worse, they may reinforce behaviour which parents do not want to see in their children. One of us tried to teach behavioural methods to his mother. He finally persuaded her that although his son's 'showing off behaviour' amused her as being 'cute', it did not evoke the same response in others, especially his parents!

Similarly, few parents or teachers seem to realize that they can often bring tantrum troubles upon themselves. How often have we observed an incident like the following in a shopping centre. A toddler passing a shop window with a parent sees a toy and shouts, 'I wannit, I wannit!' The parent says, 'Not today dear' and moves on. The child stays behind, begins to cry and kick and repeat the demand more volubly. The parent again refuses and there follows a series of increasingly vociferous demands, each followed by refusal. At this point the parent may smack the child in desperation, which can result in a tearful screamings. The parent, embarrassed by the noise and the looks of the passers-by (nearly all of whom sympathize with the child) eventually gives in and buys the child the toy. The child stops crying, beams triumphantly and the parent is only too glad that the incident is over. Unfortunately, the problem has only just begun. The parent has quite definitely positively reinforced the screaming and demanding by giving the child the toy. (Incidentally, the child has negatively reinforced the parent's compliance by learning to scream and demand until he gets the toy.) The next time they go shopping the same situation is more likely to occur as the child has learned that screaming in public brings 'goodies', or that long term 'pestering' will eventually bring a reward. The parent has learned that giving in will reduce tantrums.

The best solution to this problem is not to reinforce demanding behaviour in the first place. However, given that the problem already exists one remedy is to employ an extinction procedure and to withhold reinforcement by refusing to buy goodies in such situations. But this is more difficult than it seems. It may take a long time and a great deal of noisy protesting, perhaps even louder than it was at first, before the child learns that these behaviours will not be reinforced. Ingenious parents will make goodies contingent upon good behaviour during the shopping trip, i.e. children will only receive goodies at the end if they behave satisfactorily. Parents might also, however, sensibly use praise to reinforce continuing good behaviour during the trip. If parents later only reinforce occasionally, then they will not only save money spent on goodies but will also have helped the child learn appropriate behaviour. A simple booklet for parents detailing behavioural procedures like these is available, entitled *Seven Supertactics for Superparents* (Wheldall, Wheldall and Winter, 1983).

While toys or sweets are fairly safe bets as reinforcers for most very young children, it may prove worthwhile to determine or define more appropriate reinforcers. We should remember that reinforcers can be defined as any consequence which increases the probability of that behaviour. Skinner has also suggested that what an individual will 'go for' is also a good indicator of a reinforcer. This is very useful in practice, as is an extension of this idea known as the Premack principle or, colloquially, as 'grandma's rule'; for example, 'you can go out to play after you've done the chores.' Specifically, this principle states that a more frequent behaviour can be used to reinforce a less frequent behaviour by making the more frequent behaviour contingent upon the performance of the less frequent behaviour. Secondary-school teachers employ this principle when they make access to a preferred activity, such as drama, contingent upon children completing a less preferred activity, such as writing an essay.

In determining reinforcers, the golden rule is 'if it works use it' (within reason!). The most unlikely things can sometimes prove reinforcing; on the other hand, some 'obvious' reinforcers may not always work. It is important to remember that reinforcers are defined by their consequences – do they increase behaviour(s) or not? Reinforcers for use in primary school might include activities such as being allowed to water the plants or to ring the bell for morning break, looking after the noticeboards or the class library, answering the telephone or feeding the guinea pigs. Reinforcers for use in secondary schools might include a few minutes free time, choice of activities within a lesson, choice of seating arrangements, access to extra-curricular activities, or a positive letter home from the teachers.

Some years ago we were working with a non-verbal four year old – Tim. He had a simple understanding of language but no speech. His difficulty had been compounded by his mother, who had 'spoilt him' by continually giving in to his gestural or grunted demands and not requiring verbal requests from him. Tim controlled his mother. The balance of power in this interaction was entirely on Tim's side. Tim's behaviours were rather idiosyncratic and we had problems finding appropriate reinforcers. Smarties were no good – he would accept them only occasionally, only when given by his mother and only out of a small tube and not from a large box! Observation of his play, however, revealed his passion for jigsaws. So we used his more frequent jigsaw play to shape up less frequent language behaviour. This proved highly effective. Another interesting point about Tim was his reaction to jelly which has often been found to be a convenient, easily dispensed, easily consumed and powerful reinforcer for children with severe intellectual disabilities. For Tim, however, jelly proved to be an aversive stimulus. What is reinforcing for one child is not necessarily reinforcing for another. A teacher skilled in the behavioural approach will make a point of knowing his or her pupils well enough to appreciate what each will find reinforcing.

When we want to teach children to learn something new, or to encourage them to behave in a certain way more frequently than they normally do, it is important that we ensure that they are positively reinforced frequently for behaving appropriately. This normally leads to rapid learning. When children have learned the new behaviour and/or are behaving appropriately on a regular basis, then we may maintain this behaviour more economically by reducing the frequency of reinforcement. Another important reason for wanting to reduce the frequency is that children may become less responsive if the positive reinforcers become too easily available. Consequently, once children are regularly behaving in an appropriate way we can best maintain that behaviour by ensuring that they are now reinforced only intermittently.

Employing Reinforcement Selectively

Discussion among teachers and educators who are familiar with the notion of positive reinforcement typically centres around two issues. The first concerns the relative merits of particular reinforcers (e.g. is time at a chosen activity a more educationally acceptable or ethically defensible rewarding event than earned points which are exchanged for consumable items, such as sweets?). The second issue concerns practical procedures or techniques for administering reinforcement – e.g. the use of star charts, contract cards, token economies or pupil self-recording of rewards. While both the choice of appropriate reinforcing events and the devising of practical procedures for implementing reinforcement in the classroom are important, extensive concern with these issues often precludes consideration of a prior and educationally more important issue of contingency. What behaviour is reinforcement to be contingent upon?

Technical decisions concerning the selection, scheduling and implementation of reinforcement are less important for teachers than decisions concerning which behaviours qualify for reinforcement. There are four principles, emerging from our previous research, which can guide teachers in making these decisions. These principles, which are elaborated at several points in this book, may be summarized as follows. Teachers employing a behavioural interactionist approach should ensure that children are reinforced i) for appropriate behaviour and not for inappropriate behaviour; ii) for both academic and attentive (on-task) behaviour; iii) for fluent, rather than merely accurate, behaviour, and iv) for independent, rather than dependent, behaviour.

One of the major contributions of early applied behavioural research in classrooms was the consistent demonstration that positive reinforcement in the form of teacher attention to appropriate behaviour not only increased children's appropriate behaviour, but also clearly decreased inappropriate behaviour. Indeed, the strategy of 'catch the children being good' (Madsen, Becker and Thomas, 1968) has become a basic component of behavioural programmes for classroom management, as we will see. Most teachers would insist that teacher praise for appropriate child behaviour is an elementary and commonplace teaching practice. There is growing evidence to suggest, however, that this may not be the case, as the findings presented in the next chapter will show.

Successful use of teacher approval for appropriate classroom behaviour depends on successful observation of appropriate behaviour. Teachers need both clear specifications of behaviour that is appropriate to the task, and skills in observing and detecting this behaviour. Even greater skill is needed in observation and detection when a child displays only a low rate of appropriate behaviour. Without these prior skills of observing and detecting appropriate behaviour the application of reinforcement will be clearly ineffective. It may result, for example, in an increased overall rate of teacher attention or praise. But this could be counter-productive, since such non-contingent attention may unintentionally reinforce inappropriate behaviours. The crucial skill for teachers employing a behavioural approach is to ensure that reinforcement (in whatever form) is delivered contingent upon observable appropriate behaviour, and that unintentional reinforcement of inappropriate behaviour is minimized.

Statements about educational goals frequently refer to the desirability of students becoming autonomous 'self-monitoring' learners, capable of acting independently of adults. Unfortunately, school management policies, particularly those relating to school rules and discipline, do not provide many opportunities for student autonomous or independent behaviour to occur. Nor do they provide sufficient reinforcement when such behaviour does occur. Within the individual classroom, independent learning can occur only to the extent that there are sufficient opportunities to perform academic behaviours outside the direct control of the teacher. Classroom organizations which allow pupils a choice of instructional activities can free the teacher to provide individual children with brief periods of one-to-one interaction. While the teacher is engaged with individual children, the remaining children can readily learn to monitor their own behaviour.

The frequently occurring one-to-one setting in which a child performs an academic skill and interacts with a teacher, however briefly, is an important context for the learning of self-regulated or independent learning. Children learning both to monitor their own behaviour and to correct their own responding are powerfully influenced by the behaviour of the teacher within the one-to-one setting and by the selection of appropriate learning materials. The teacher's use of reinforcement procedures is critical in this one-to-one context. First, it is important to recognize that an appropriately selected academic task produces its own reinforcement. Solving a problem or correctly reading a sentence produces reinforcement in the form of information. Additional or 'back-up' reinforcement may be superfluous, and may even be restricting given the previous discussion of contingencies for academic behaviour.

The selective use of reinforcement will influence not only the 'quantity' of learning taking place but also its 'quality'. In other words, the changes we are advocating will not only result in children learning skills more effectively and efficiently and gaining knowledge at a more rapid rate, but the ways in which they learn will also be changed. Conventional methods of instruction all too frequently, if unwittingly, foster dependence of the pupil on the teacher, whereas the behavioural methods outlined in this book are characterized by a desire to share control of learning with pupils themselves. Teacher-directed instruction should give way to pupil-initiated learning. Far from being at odds with so-called child-centred pedagogy, our behavioural approach assists the translation of rhetoric into reality.

Following this description of the ABC model, we can now begin to apply behavioural principles to the study of teaching. With some children the behaviour that concerns us has not yet been learned. With others the behaviour has been learned but does not occur frequently enough. Other children frequently behave in inappropriate ways. A behavioural approach to teaching is about changing the frequencies of behaviour. It can be used to teach new skills or to increase or decrease existing rates of behaviour. We believe that a behavioural interactionist approach to teaching should be primarily concerned with increasing the frequency of appropriate and educationally sound behaviours in the classroom, rather than simply decreasing disruptive behaviour or increasing conforming or dependent behaviours.

As we have said, in order to do this teachers may have to change aspects of their own behaviour. But first, we will look briefly at what we already know about how teachers normally behave in the classroom. The information we have available so far is limited; but we have carried out research studies which are beginning to inform us about the frequency with which teachers display certain key behaviours. In the following chapter, we will review our findings so far on teachers' classroom behaviour and discuss the extent to which the ways teachers usually behave is congruent with a behavioural interactionist approach. Some aspects of this may surprise you.

4

How Do Teachers Behave?

Many teachers, on first hearing about behavioural approaches to teaching, understandably react by saying: 'But that's what we do already!' And, to a certain extent this is true. It seems unlikely that many teachers are employing behavioural techniques effectively, however, otherwise there would be fewer harassed teachers! The confusion arises as a result of teachers sometimes dismissing the behavioural approach as 'obvious' or 'common sense', without paying sufficient attention to certain key principles which underpin the whole system. The techniques advocated are indeed very similar, if not identical, to the procedures utilized by many skilled teachers; nor is this surprising since few children would learn very much that is useful and desirable if these principles were not sometimes being followed.

But there are differences which it is easy to gloss over in a spirit of self-righteousness. The most important of these is undoubtedly consistency. How many teachers could put their hands on their hearts and claim to reinforce appropriate behaviours and to ignore undesirable behaviours consistently? Nor is this a cause for shame, since few teachers have been trained to do so, but this is one of the keys to success, as we shall see. One cannot expect to achieve success with the behavioural approach unless the principles are followed consistently.

Another bone of contention is the nature of reinforcement. How many teachers actually enthusiastically reinforce desired behaviours, rather than giving a begrudging tick or a 'that's OK'? Remember the teacher does not define the reinforcer – it defines itself by its effect on behaviour. It could be that you, the teacher, are not a very powerful source of social reinforcement since you have little to offer the child. It is comforting to believe that your approval is desired and is reinforcing, but is it? Ask yourself whose approval is valued by the children in your school and attempt to determine why. What have you got to offer children that will make your approval desirable? In other words you should attempt to build up your approval into a powerful social reinforcer by pairing it with known desirable consequences (existing reinforcers), i.e. make sure you become associated with events which your children really 'go for'.

What about immediacy of reinforcement? Do you wait until the end of the week to tell Janet that her writing has improved? Delay between the behaviour and the presentation of the reinforcer has been shown to weaken its effect. Similarly, are you structuring the classroom situation so as to encourage desirable behaviour to occur – by re-arranging the seating, for example? These points are raised to serve as reminders of the sort of care needed to teach effectively using the behavioural approach. No one is claiming that it is an easy or foolproof method. It is dependent upon skills being learned so well that they become automatic; skills which it is unlikely that you were taught at college, or which were not presented there within a cohesive conceptual framework. A behavioural approach is one that is well worth studying and a programme of skills well worth learning. While it does not provide you with a curriculum of what to teach, it does provide you with the means of effective teaching.

In this chapter, we will examine some of the research which informs us about how teachers typically behave in the classroom. Drawing on the results of our observational studies carried out over the years we will then be in a position to see how far it is true for teachers to say: 'Ah, but we do that already.'

TEACHERS USE OF PRAISE AND DISAPPROVAL

Behavioural approaches to teaching commonly advocate increasing teacher approval and decreasing disapproval since it has frequently been demonstrated that teacher approval can function as a powerful reinforcer of children's behaviour. This is true not only for primary-aged children but also for young people attending secondary schools. In the chapters which follow we will present examples of successful interventions carried out in both primary- and secondary- aged classes which will bear this out. Relatively little is known, however, about the ways in which approval and disapproval are normally employed in classrooms, especially in the UK and New Zealand. Almost all of the research in this area has been carried out in North America.

Brophy (1981) has made the point that praise may or may not function as a reinforcer and that teachers may employ praise for purposes other than reinforcement. This is undoubtedly, true but we know that praise can function as a reinforcer when used in a careful and systematic way. When observing teacher behaviour in the classroom, however, it is very difficult to make this sort of distinction, about whether praise delivered is reinforcing or not, in any objective way. What we can do is to sample overall use of praise (and disapproval) and to bear these reservations in mind when we consider our results.

The earliest study conducted specifically to determine natural rates of teacher approval and disapproval appears to be that of White (1975) in the United States. Under White's guidance 16 observational studies were carried out involving 104 teachers. White showed that, with the exception of those who were teaching grades one and two, American teachers gave more disapproving than approving comments to their pupils, with overall rates declining as pupils got older. Approval rate for children's academic behaviour was higher in all grades than the rate for disapproval; but for children's social behaviour, disapproval was 12 times higher than approval. Heller and White (1975) subsequently observed five teachers of mathematics and five teachers of social studies in grades seven to nine (i.e. secondary-aged classes). Mean rates of disapproval were again found to exceed mean rates of teacher approval, and out of a total of 1,105 statements of approval and disapproval recorded, only one was found to be approving of social behaviour! Following up this research, Russell and Lin (1977) in South Australia found evidence to suggest that the worst-behaved pupils in the class received more negative than positive teacher attention, whereas the best-behaved children received more positive than negative attention.

Brophy (1981) reviewed six separate studies of 'teacher praise and criticism of student behaviour.' The findings overall consistently indicated that teachers were more likely to praise appropriate academic behaviour than to criticize it, but were more likely to show disapproval of academic behaviour than to praise good conduct.

Nafpaktitis, Mayer and Butterworth (1985), in a study involving nearly 90 teachers of grades six to nine, found that the amount of disruptive and off-task pupil behaviour was clearly related to teacher use of approval and disapproval. Lower rates of disruptive and off-task behaviours were mildly associated with higher rates of appropriate approval while teacher disapproval correlated positively with both disruptive and non-task pupil behaviours. It is interesting to note that the researchers also found a larger positive correlation between inappropriate teacher approval and pupil disruptive behaviour. In other words, higher rates of teacher approval to off-task behaviours were associated with higher rates of pupil disruptive behaviour. Overall, the teachers in this study gave more appropriate approving responses than disapproving responses.

In the UK the main sources of relevant data, apart from our own research, are the ORACLE study of interaction in 58 top-junior British classrooms (Galton, Simon and Croll, 1980) and, at the secondary level, the 'fifteen thousand hours' study of Rutter, Maughan, Mortimore and Ouston (1979). Neither of these studies had as its central focus, teachers' 'natural' use of approval and disapproval, but relevant findings on this issue emerged from these research projects. The ORACLE team found that statements relating to classroom behaviour ('critical control') were twice as frequent as praise statements relating to academic work, and that the most frequent type of teacher utterance recorded was 'neutral or critical feedback on work or effort'. On average, pupils received ten times as much criticism for inappropriate social behaviour as praise for good work.

Rutter, Maughan, Mortimore and Ouston studied 12 secondary schools in inner London with the aim of 'collecting fairly simple descriptive data about lessons'. Their observation schedule allowed data to be collected on both teacher and pupil behaviour. They found that secondary-aged children were on-task about 80 per cent of the time. Rates of teacher approval and disapproval appeared to show that frequent disciplining interventions in the classroom were associated with worse behaviour. The absolute rates of teacher praise to pupils' work were very low, usually only three or four instances per lesson. However, those schools in which praise in lessons was most frequent tended to be the schools in which better behaviour and lower delinquency rates were evident. Frequent public praise for good work or behaviour by commending individual pupils in assembly or other meetings was also associated with better pupil behaviour.

Over the last ten years or so we too have carried out research studies in this area in both New Zealand and the UK. Our first, small-scale study was completed in New Zealand (Thomas, Presland, Grant and Glynn, 1978). We observed the classroom behaviour of ten grade-seven teachers in schools serviced by the Mangere Guidance Unit, a behavioural-support-team facility serving three intermediate schools. A time-sampling instrument was used to record teacher behaviours and the on-task behaviour level of a sample of ten pupils from each class. Results similar to those of White (1975) were obtained, showing that the majority of teachers displayed rates of disapproval higher than approval rates. Moreover, seven of the ten teachers had disapproval rates at least three times greater than their approval rates. Appropriate behaviour in these classrooms ranged from 43 to 90 per cent, the lowest score being that of one class whose teacher had a ratio of disapproval to approval of 17 to 1. Caution must be expressed at these findings, however, since the Mangere Unit is an innovative educational facility providing essentially an in-service support role which caters for a sample of pupils of similar age with behavioural difficulties and their teachers. The data gathered in this unit both justified and provided a basis for within school staff development programmes. These programmes included assisting teachers to reduce their rate of attention to inappropriate pupil behaviour and to increase their rate of attention to appropriate behaviour.

We subsequently observed a much larger sample of 128 British primary- and middle-school teachers to see if their behaviour was similar to that of their counterparts in New Zealand, Australia and the United States (Merrett and Wheldall, 1987a). The OPTIC schedule, described briefly in the last chapter, was developed as part of this research. We wanted to collect information on the on-task behaviour of the classes observed as well as on teachers' use of approval and disapproval for academic work and classroom social behaviour separately. Each teacher and class were observed on at least three separate occasions for 30 minutes each time.

An analysis of the data revealed total rates of approval (56%) as higher than total disapproval (44%), with more teacher responses given to academic work (66%) than to classroom social behaviours (34%). In terms of academic behaviours alone, positive teacher responses occurred three times more frequently than negative responses, whereas for social behaviours alone, negative responses were five times more frequent than positive responses. Of the 128 teachers observed, 38 of them *never* expressed any approval towards social behaviour, while six of them each gave over 20 such responses, clearly reflecting the variability between teachers. The pupils in the classes observed were found to be on-task for an average of 70% of the time.

British primary school teachers, then, in general *approve* slightly more than they *disapprove*, contrary to the findings from overseas. In fact, approval for academic behaviour ('Well done John, what neat handwriting') is much higher than disapproval ('Only two sums right, not very good, eh Susan?'). But for *social* behaviour the reverse is the case. Teachers are very quick to notice social behaviour of which they disapprove and continually nag children about it. ('Sharon, how many more times do I have to tell you to stay in your seat?') But they hardly ever approve of desirable social behaviour ('That's how I like it class; you have been sharing the art materials without any arguments'). In other words, children are expected to behave well and are continually reprimanded if they do not.

The next, obvious step was to carry out a similar large-scale observational study on secondary-school teachers and their classes (Wheldall, Houghton and Merrett, 1989), again using OPTIC. The subjects of this observational study consisted of 130 secondary-school teachers and their (mixed) classes. The sample comprised 63 female and 67 male teachers, varying in age and teaching the full range of academic subjects, with the exception of physical education, games, dance and drama. All age groups of pupils taught (years one to five) were observed in this study. The age of the classes observed varied between 11–12 years of age and 16 years of age, with between 7 and 50 classes observed at each age level.

For this sample, overall approval (55%) was again higher than overall disapproval (45%), and more comments were made in response to academic behaviours (59%) than to social behaviours (41%). For academic behaviours alone, positive responses were three times as frequent as negative responses, but for social behaviours, negative responses were three times as frequent as positive responses. Considerable variability was evident in teacher behaviours; for example, approval to social behaviour was *never* expressed by 26 of the 130 teachers, while 7 of them each gave over 20 such responses. The mean percentage on-task behaviour of the classes observed was about 80% which suggests, in so far as this sample is representative, that British secondary school pupils spend a very high percentage of their time engaged in activities defined as appropriate by their teachers.

It appears, then, that secondary teachers are also quick to detect incidents of which they disapprove, yet they rarely approve or comment upon desirable or appropriate social behaviours. A common, widely held feeling among teachers is that pupils are expected to behave themselves and therefore need no praise or comment for conforming to the 'rules'.

It is interesting to speculate why teachers make so many disapproving comments. Heller and White (1975) suggested that teachers may find use of disapproval more reinforcing than the use of approval. We suspect that disapproval comments may be maintained because it is reinforcing to the teacher to detect inappropriate behaviour.

Disapproval comments may also be reinforced through their possible short-term effect in terminating inappropriate behaviour. However, such a strategy will not necessarily result in any increase in appropriate child behaviour; indeed increasing teacher attention to inappropriate behaviour may even increase this behaviour, as we shall see.

TEACHERS' USE OF TOUCH IN EARLY CHILDHOOD EDUCATION

Children are clearly influenced by what teachers say, but they are also influenced by teachers' non-verbal communications. We have been particularly interested in teachers' use of touch. Casual observation suggested that teachers of young children (nursery- and infant-school teachers) touched the children in their classes fairly frequently, and we were interested to know what functions touch served in early-childhood education. Two of our studies (reported in the following chapter) had provided evidence in support of touch as a powerful reinforcer for young children's classroom behaviour. We wanted to know the extent to which teachers used touch functionally, and in particular whether touch was used 'naturally' as a reinforcer.

In a review of research into the role of non-verbal communication in the classroom, Smith (1979) refers to over 80 studies but only one of these referred to teacher touch behaviour. Our own literature searches also revealed very few further studies. Teacher touch behaviour is clearly an under-researched area, references to teacher touch often being merely anecdotal or speculative. The few studies that have actually explored the use of touch in an experimental or empirical manner have, for the most part, been carried out in the United States. Pratt (1973) and Heinig (1976) carried out studies examining the effect of teacher touch on children's reading achievements but report no significant differences between children who received tactile contact and those who did not. Perdue and Connor (1978) observed the patterns of touching between pre-school children (aged between three and five years) and male and female teachers. They found that teachers touched children of their own sex more frequently than children of the opposite sex. Clements and Tracey (1977) reported that touch used as positive reinforcement for children's learning and classroom behaviour was most successful in combination with verbal cues.

Research in British classrooms is even more limited, apart from our own research. We decided to follow up our earlier experimental work on touch as a reinforcer (see chapter 6) and to gather further observational data on the general use of teacher touch behaviour in order to begin to document the role that touch plays in classroom communication. We developed a version of the OPTIC observation schedule which included categories of touch and a system of recording the body area touched. This allowed us to observe teachers and to record the amount and type of touch used in nursery and infant classrooms. Our aim was to determine whether teacher touch behaviour (in kind and amount) varied according to the age and gender of children taught, and also to relate functions of touch to body area touched. (Bevan and Wheldall, 1985).

We observed 36 female teachers in their respective early-childhood education settings (nursery, reception and post-reception classes). All the schools were situated in and around an industrial town in the West Midlands. Each of the 36 teachers was observed on three separate occasions for 30 minutes each time. There was wide variation over the 36 teachers in the frequency of use of teacher touch. Surprisingly, there were no significant differences in the amount of touch behaviour observed between the nursery, reception and post-reception class teachers. (It is possible, however, that nursery-aged children do receive more touch but that this is given mainly by nursery nurses.) Similarly, there were no differences between boys and girls at any age level in the amount of touch they received.

Our findings on parts of the body touched show that the head, being easily accessible, is touched most often. This is quite an important finding as some ethnic and cultural sub-groups find this offensive. This is certainly the case for New Zealand Maori and some Polynesian groups. In the nursery and reception classes in our study, hands were touched frequently since very young children often need considerable physical guidance. The shoulders and back are other areas of the body which are easily accessible and therefore touched fairly frequently. It would seem that there was no particular significance in the part of the body touched beyond that of ease of accessibility.

The apparent functions of teacher touch were similar for all three age groups of children taught. Teacher touch was mainly used for no apparent reason ('other'; 33%), for 're-direction' (29%) and for 'instruction' (22%). Touch is sometimes used for disapproving of social behaviour (10%) but is hardly ever used to accompany praise or disapproval for academic behaviour (4% and 1% respectively) and is almost never employed to praise appropriate social behaviour (less than 1%). This is particularly interesting in view of our findings about the use of touch as a reinforcer, reported in chapter 6. There are, quite literally, very few pats on the back.

THE AMOUNT OF TIME CHILDREN SPEND WAITING FOR THE TEACHER

Informal discussions with infant-school heads and class teachers suggested that a common classroom management problem, experienced by many teachers, was the amount of time children spent waiting for assistance from their teacher. This was an aspect of teacher behaviour about which, again, there is very little published information. Consequently we decided to carry out an observational study (West and Wheldall, 1988) to provide more objective information on the ways in which infant-class teachers dealt with requests for attention and how long children had to wait for this attention.

A sample of 20 British female infant school teachers and their classes was observed, selected (as far as possible) to include a range of catchment areas and types of school in the West Midlands. Eleven top- and nine middle-infant classes were observed. Each class teacher agreed to have an observer present for four 30-minute sessions.

Data were collected by scanning the class at one minute intervals and counting the number of boys and girls (separately) waiting for attention from the teacher and whether they were sitting with a hand raised or queuing at the teacher's desk. (From our pilot studies it was clear that most teachers used a procedure either of children coming to them for help i.e. 'queueing' or of the teacher going to the child i.e. 'hands-up'.) Since the numerical count at each timed interval would not give any indication of the waiting time for any single child, a system of timing individual children by stop-watch was also incorporated.

On average, about three children were observed to be waiting at any one time, varying from zero to 21 children waiting in classes of approximately 30 children. Half of the teachers usually had fewer than two children waiting, but one-fifth of teachers had four or more children, on average, waiting for attention at any one time. There was very little difference between the mean numbers of boys and girls waiting, but the mean number of children waiting rose as the lesson progressed. The mean length of time spent waiting was about one-and-a-half minutes, but this was highly variable, ranging from zero (when children received immediate attention) to over 13 minutes. This should be appreciated in the context of the length of the observation period, 30 minutes. A quarter of the teachers were observed to have had at least one child in their class waiting for more than ten minutes. These same classes also had *mean* waiting times greater than one-and-a-half minutes. One teacher had children waiting for over four minutes on average but nine of the 20 teachers usually kept children waiting for less than a minute. Although marginally more children were recorded waiting under queueing procedures than under hands-up procedures, the hands-up procedure resulted in more than twice as much waiting time as the queue procedure and more children abandoned waiting for teacher attention altogether.

A child of infant-school age is unlikely to be able to work continuously throughout the day and, therefore, an interruption of around one-and-a-half minutes, to secure teacher attention, might be supposed to be reasonable. However, the data showed that in five of the 20 classrooms the waiting time exceeded ten minutes. This cannot be regarded as satisfactory practice. Similarly, a total of 21 children out of a class of 27 all waiting for teacher help at the same time, as occurred in one case, is a cause for concern.

Queueing proved to be more efficient than the hands-up system of signalling in terms of the length of time children had to wait for teacher attention, but 'hands-up' may be preferable from a classroom management point of view, since it involves more teacher movement around the room. Teachers who move systematically from table to table are better able to monitor children's work. One possibility is to use a mobile-queue system, where the teacher moves from table to table and children needing help queue and move with her. This method incorporates the best feature of the queueing procedure (a shorter waiting time for children), while at the same time allowing the teacher to monitor the work of individuals or groups of children. However, since classrooms are such complex systems involving so many variables, the relative effectiveness of these procedures needs to be evaluated experimentally, and further research is proceeding along these lines.

LISTENING TO CHILDREN READ

It is generally agreed that teachers listening to children read is sound educational practice. Teachers of young children certainly spend considerable amounts of time doing it. For example, research carried out for the Bullock Report (1975) involving 936 primary schools found that more than 50 per cent of teachers of six-year olds listened to all of their pupils read at least three times per week. But whether it is particularly effective in helping young children learn to read or whether it is merely ritualistic, as some critics have suggested, is difficult to determine since there is relatively little research on what teachers actually do when they hear children read to them, or on its effects.

Our research studies were conducted with the aim of determining whether teachers typically tutor naturally in ways consonant with tutoring practices we currently advocate. More specifically, our studies sought to determine whether the 'Pause, Prompt and Praise' tutoring procedures (which will be described in detail in chapter 8) were commonly employed by teachers listening to children read. 'Pause, Prompt and Praise' (McNaughton, Glynn and Robinson, 1987) is a set of tutoring procedures for reading designed for older low-progress readers. In essence, tutors are required to learn to pause before responding to a child's error, to offer prompts rather than supply correct words, and to praise specifically for independent reading behaviour. Evidence suggests that these procedures are very effective. When teachers and other educationists are informed of these procedures they often claim, yet again, that 'of course, we do that already.'

Some of the research literature on this topic (for example, Gumperz and Hernandez-Chavez, 1972) suggests that teachers respond differently to high- and low-progress readers. They are more likely to make an immediate interruption to a low-progress reader's error, and the error is more likely to be treated in isolation rather than related to a wider meaning context. Allington (1980) and McNaughton (1978) found that poor readers were interrupted immediately on about three quarters of their mistakes. The most common response was to tell them the correct word immediately. There is mounting research evidence to show that poor readers are treated differentially by teachers in ways which make it more difficult, not less difficult, for them to progress.

In our original 'Pause, Prompt and Praise' development project carried out in New Zealand (McNaughton, Glynn and Robinson, 1987), detailed data were obtained on five classroom teachers listening to older low-progress children read. On average, ten tape-recordings per teacher were analysed. The results showed that, on average, these teachers responded to a high rate of children's errors (74%) but paused before responding for only 34% of the errors. Praise rates were surprisingly low, averaging about four per session.

Subsequently we decided to observe three distinct groups of teachers and readers in the UK: a sample of 55 teachers listening to low-progress readers in upper-junior, middle and lower-secondary classes in mainstream schools; a sample of 31 teachers listening to secondary-aged pupils in special schools for children with moderate learning difficulties; and finally a sample of 55 teachers in junior-infant and first schools listening to children in the early stages of learning to read. This research is reported fully in Wheldall, Wenban-Smith, Morgan and Quance (1988).

In all three studies, teachers were told that we were interested in how children performed when reading aloud to their teachers. The role of the teacher in the interaction was not stressed so as to encourage natural teacher responding. Teachers were asked simply to select a child and to hear that child read from where he or she had finished reading on the previous occasion. Teachers asked the child to read the next 100 words from his or her reading book. Each reading interaction was tape-recorded and subsequently analysed.

Analyses of the data suggested that teachers, on average, attended to about 80–90% of children's reading errors and that this was similar for all three groups. Very little of this attention to errors, however, was delayed by more than five seconds; in fact half of the teachers never 'paused' at all. Whereas for the young average-progress and older low-progress readers teachers paused at the low rate of about 20%, for the very low-progress readers teachers paused at the even lower rate of 5%! About 65% of errors were followed by 'prompts' (rather than providing the correct word) for both groups of delayed readers, and about 50% of errors by young average readers received prompts. Such prompts generally resulted in children correcting the word about three-quarters of the time. Teachers praised, on average, only about three times per session, and this was usually very general, non-specific praise. An important additional finding was that over 50% of children were reading from books which were generally too easy for them to make much progress. This is an example of a setting event (text difficulty) limiting the academic learning which can take place. We advocate criteria for book level selection which avoid using books that are too difficult but also avoid using books that are so easy that no errors occur, since errors provide important opportunities for learning. (We shall return to this point in chapter 8.)

Once again, then, we find that teachers are not using simple behavioural teaching methods 'naturally'. The picture builds up of teachers failing to make the most of opportunities which arise for helping children to learn more effective strategies for independent learning. We know that teachers at all levels do not often use praise to reinforce appropriate social behaviour in the classroom. We know that infant-class teachers seldom use touch to accompany praise and that they frequently keep children waiting for teacher attention. We also know that when hearing children read, teachers correct almost all errors immediately, seldom give praise, and select texts at inappropriate levels of difficulty. In a sense, this is the bad news; the good news is that teachers can readily learn to change to more positive, behavioural teaching approaches. The further good news is that children can also change in response to changed teacher behaviour, so that more effective learning can occur.

5

Classroom Seating Arrangements

When we first started school in the early 1950s, we sat with our peers in one of several rows of double desks facing the blackboard and the teacher's desk. (One of us also claims to be one of the last to be issued with a slate and chalk, but that is another story!) But when our children started school, in the 1970s, they were seated around tables. When we and our children went on to secondary school, however, we found ourselves, from the first day, seated in rows.

What had happened in the intervening years to bring about this change in primary-classroom seating arrangements? The answer, of course, was the move towards more child-centred education, endorsed in Britain by the influential Plowden Report (Department of Education and Science, 1967). This government report, on *Children and Their Primary Schools*, had a rapid and major impact on certain aspects of primary school practice. Without referring to any supporting empirical evidence, the Plowden Report urged the replacement of rows with table groups since the received wisdom was that effective learning could take place only under conditions of continued peer interaction.

The Plowden Report argued that children should be seated in groups to help in the socialization process. Apparently as a result, the slower members of the group would be helped through interaction with the more able. 'Apathetic' children would be 'infected by the enthusiasm of the group', and interaction would also benefit more able children through the 'cut and counterthrust of conversation' and the 'opportunities to teach as well as to learn' (para. 757). So potent was the heady brew distilled by Plowden that the educational establishment became a little 'high' on the spirit of idealism. 'Discovery learning' was on almost every primary teacher's lips, and table groups displaced rows in the vast majority of classrooms. But as in so many things in life, 'when all is said and done, more was said than done.'

There is no doubt that the aims of Plowden were in tune with sound educational philosophy (and the child-centred approach is certainly in line with a behavioural interactionist perspective, as we noted earlier). Putting these ideas into practice was another matter. Some of the more superficial changes were readily made, so that schools looked more 'progressive', but underneath, relatively little had changed. It was not enough just to change the seating, teaching behaviours and curriculum content had to change along with it.

Boydell (1974, 1975) has suggested that it might be more difficult than is generally supposed to set up group working conditions as envisaged in the Plowden Report. Plowden argued that seating in groups would help children to learn to get along together, enable them to help one another and help them realize their own strengths and weaknesses; but the results of Boydell's research suggested that sustained conversations in which children explain and develop their ideas and suggestions may be relatively unknown. Only half of the conversations, according to Boydell, concerned children's work, and most were of less than 25 seconds' duration. She suggested that children were more likely to be work orientated when they were *not* interacting than when they were. More recently, the 'ORACLE' research of Galton, Simon and Croll (1980) showed that while the tables formation was the most common setting in junior schools, individual, non-collaborative work-tasks remained the norm in these schools. It is hardly surprising, then, that Boydell, and also Bennett, Desforges, Cockburn and Wilkinson (1984), found that a large part of the social interaction observed in table groups was non-work-related. Setting individual tasks based, say, on a series of work cards is not really conducive to collaborative effort and for such activities it may even be counter-productive to seat children in groups around tables.

In this chapter we will examine the effects of classroom seating arrangements on both children's and teachers' behaviour. As we said earlier, enduring antecedent events may be divided into ecological variables and setting events. Seating arrangements are some of the most influential ecological variables affecting classroom behaviour, and can also be relatively easily altered by the classroom teacher. From a behavioural interactionist perspective we, as teachers, need to know the effects of such powerful ecological variables so that we can structure our classrooms to provide effective contexts for the learning-tasks we have set. For different tasks and activities we may well need to organize different seating arrangements. In the following chapter we will consider behavioural approaches to managing classroom social behaviour; as we shall see, making use of such ecological factors as seating arrangements can help us at least part of the way in this endeavour.

CHANGING CLASSROOM BEHAVIOUR BY CHANGING FROM TABLES TO ROWS

The literature concerning classroom seating arrangements and their effects on children's learning and classroom behaviour goes back over 50 years (see Wheldall, Morris, Vaughan and Ng, 1981 for a review). Studies were carried out by Griffith in 1921 and Dawe in 1934 on the relationship between seating position and academic performance. More recent studies on class seating arrangements include those by Krantz and Risley (1977), Axelrod, Hall and Tams (1979) and our own research.

Krantz and Risley demonstrated that kindergarten children's classroom behaviour can be changed by systematically varying how close children were to each other. They found that children attended to their teacher more when they were placed with a space between each child and his or her neighbours during story-time than when they were allowed to cluster together around the teacher. Their study also showed that this strategy was just as effective in reducing disruptions as a positive reinforcement procedure which involved rewarding with praise and privileges, while being easier and quicker to employ. This is a good example of the power of ecological variables in classroom behaviour management.

Our own reseach was inspired by the work of Axelrod and his colleagues in the United States. They compared the effects of two classroom seating arrangments, tables versus rows, on the on-task and disruptive behaviour of two classes of children. In their first study, involving a class of 17 seven- to eight-year olds from an inner-city elementary school, the on-task behaviour of the class was observed daily while the pupils independently completed formal academic work. On-task behaviour averaged 62% during the nine-day baseline phase when children were seated at tables, but increased by 20%, to a mean of 82% when the children were moved from groups to being seated in rows for ten days. When the class went back to tables for seven days, average on-task behaviour fell back to 63%, but again rose to 83% when seating in rows was resumed for the final seven-day phase. Similarly, in the second study involving a class of 32 twelve- to thirteen-year olds, disruptive 'talk-outs' were shown to decrease markedly during seating in rows compared with seating at tables.

Consequently, we embarked upon a series of studies to investigate this particular ecological variable more thoroughly to see if we could replicate these findings in a different cultural teaching context from that obtaining in the United States and to explore any other effects such a change in seating might bring about. First, we carried out two parallel studies comparing 'tables' and 'rows' seating arrangements in two state junior schools in the West Midlands in the UK (Wheldall, Morris, Vaughan and Ng, 1981). In both schools a fourth-year class of 10–11-year-old children was chosen. One class consisted of 28 mixed sex and mixed ability children attending a school in an urban residential area, whereas the other class consisted of 25 similar children from a school on a council housing estate. In both classes, the children usually sat around tables in groups of four, five or six. The design, procedure and, indeed, results of the two studies were very similar.

The children were initially observed for two weeks (ten school days) in their normal seating arrangements around tables. An observation schedule was employed to obtain samples of on-task behaviour. This was defined, by the teachers, as doing what the teacher instructed, i.e. looking at and listening to her when she was talking to them, looking at their books or work cards when they were required to complete set work, only being out of seats with the teacher's permission, etc. Note that the definition was based on how the teachers wanted the children to behave. In the first study, observations were made only during purely academic lessons when the children had been given individual work to complete, but in the second study observations were carried out at different times including all lessons except PE, Art and Music. Calling out, talking to neighbours and interrupting were regarded as off-task by the teachers in both studies. The observation schedule provided estimates of percentage on-task behaviour for each child for each lesson which, when averaged, gave an estimate of on-task behaviour for the whole class.

After the class was observed for two weeks sitting around tables (baseline phase), the desks/tables were moved into rows without comment from the teacher and the children were observed for a further two weeks. Finally, the desks were moved back to their original positions, again without comment, for a further two weeks of observation, completing our ABA design. This time there were a few complaints from the children since they said that they *preferred* sitting in rows.

In short, in both classes, on-task behaviour increased when the children were placed in rows and fell by nearly as much when they returned to tables. The on-task behaviour of the first class rose from an average of 72% to 85% in rows and fell back to 73% when tables seating was resumed. Similarly, the second class rose from averaging 68% on-task behaviour during baseline (tables) to 92% during rows, and fell to 73% for the final tables phase. The most marked improvements in on-task behaviour occurred within those individual children whose on-task behaviour was previously very low, i.e. below 60%. For these children, increases of 30% were not uncommon. As we might expect, the effect was smaller in the case of children with high initial on-task behaviour.

We then went on to carry out a more detailed study on seating arrangements in a special school for children with learning and behaviour problems (Wheldall and Lam, 1987). In this study, we also included observations of disruptive behaviour and teacher behaviour, using an early version of the OPTIC schedule described earlier. A great deal of data were collected in this study but we will report only the main findings here.

Three classes were observed for four phases of ten observations each, spread over approximately two-week intervals. Again, seating was usually arranged around tables. In the first phase, observations were carried out in the usual (tables) conditions to provide baseline data, followed by phase 2, in which the class was moved into rows. Phase 3 constituted a return to the tables seating arrangement, followed by phase 4, in which seating was again arranged in rows. This study extended the ABA design of the previous study to an ABAB design. All lessons took place in the same room and were maths lessons given by the same teacher to all three classes: a junior class of 11 children, a middle class of 11 children and a senior class of 12 children. For the final two phases of the study, observations were also carried out on the same classes during English lessons. In these lessons, with a different teacher, seating remained in groups (tables) throughout.

The results dramatically confirmed and extended our previous findings. For every class, on-task behaviour doubled during rows seating, from around 35% to about 70%, and fell back during tables seating conditions. Similarly, rate of disruptions trebled during tables seating and fell during rows seating. We also observed changes in teacher behaviour. Positive comments consistently went up during rows conditions while negative comments decreased. The teacher apparently found it easier to praise and to refrain from disapproval when the children were seated in rows. There were no such systematic changes in pupil or teacher behaviours during the English lessons, where seating arrangements remained unchanged.

Several more recent (as yet unpublished) studies have also been completed which attempt to answer some of the possible objections to the earlier studies. We have shown that the results are not due to a novelty effect, since on-task behaviour remains at higher levels even after many weeks of sitting in rows. Moreover, we have shown that the quantity and quality of individual work produced is also appreciably greater during rows conditions.

Bennett and Blundell (1983), following up our work, also studied the effects of tables and rows on the quantity and quality of work produced in reading, language and mathematics by two classes of 10–11-year-old children. Their results also suggested that quantity of work completed generally increased when the children were seated in rows. No increase in quality is reported, although the researchers claim that existing quality levels were maintained.

Before commenting on the practical implications of these findings, we must attempt to answer the question 'Why does seating around tables lead to more disruption, less on-task behaviour and less desirable teacher behaviour?' The answers are quite simple. Tables arrangements enhance social interaction by facilitating eye contact, a prime means of initiating a social encounter, and by providing a setting for increased participation in such encounters by involving the whole group. After all, we engineer such seating arrangements in precisely this way when we wish to encourage social interaction; in committees or when playing bridge, for example. Tables allow the opportunity for covert disruptions such as teasing, kicking or pinching under the table. Rows formations, on the other hand, minimize either form of social contact, allowing fewer instances of undesirable behaviour for the teacher to comment upon adversely, and more instances of desirable behaviour for him or her to comment upon favourably. In short, it could be argued that it amounts to little short of cruelty to place children in manifestly social contexts, expect them to work independently and then to punish them when they talk or interact.

Let us emphasize, however, that we are certainly *not* advocating a return to rows for all work. Seating in rows is one possible strategy for encouraging academic work which requires each child to concentrate on the specific task in hand without distractions.

Alternatively, it might prove to be an effective bridge for an inexperienced or apprehensive teacher to use on a short-term basis while other teaching skills are being learned, the increases in on-task behaviour also providing instances of appropriate behaviour to reinforce. Rows would be totally inappropriate, however, for small group discussions or group topic work requiring collaborative effort, where table arrangements would almost certainly prove more effective.

The point we are trying to make here is simply that seating arrangements should be taken into account, and structured and varied according to the nature of the task. Similarly, it must be appreciated that child-centred education will not come about merely by changing from rows to tables. The nature of the academic tasks we set children and the behaviour of teachers must also change. At present, in many primary classes, we may be providing one of the least effective learning contexts as a result of this mismatch between the tasks set and the seating arrangements provided. This may be what the children are trying to tell us when they say that they prefer sitting in rows.

THE EFFECTS OF MIXED AND SAME-SEX CLASSROOM SEATING ARRANGEMENTS

Few studies have been reported which consider both sex differences and seating arrangements. Our earlier studies showed that both boys' and girls' on-task behaviour was higher when they were seated in rows. As far as we know, the effects of location of boys in relation to girls in the classroom does not appear to have been investigated to any great extent. An isolated study is that of Burdett, Egner and McKenzie (1970), who found that some children worked for longer periods when boys were seated next to girls and for shorter periods when boys were seated next to other boys. Frazier and Sadler (1973), however, describing a strategy for the elimination of sexism in primary schools, advocated that boys should not be 'punished' by being forced to sit next to girls.

Most of us would advocate that, ideally, children should be given as much choice as possible as to where they sit and with whom. In those classrooms arranged in table groups this almost inevitably results in girls and boys being seated around separate tables. Similarly, in classes where children sit in rows it is almost always found that children of the same sex prefer to sit next to each other. Teachers sometimes claim, however, that one of the most effective ways of curbing the disruptive behaviour of children, particularly boys, is to sit them next to a member of the opposite sex. The aim of the following studies was to determine whether mixed-sex seating does in fact, produce such clear effects, in terms of changes in on-task behaviour.

The first of these studies (Wheldall and Olds, 1987) was carried out with a third-year class and a fourth-year class in a junior school in an inner-city area of Birmingham. The third-year class consisted of 31 mixed-ability children (16 boys, 15 girls) aged nine to ten years. The fourth-year class consisted of 25 academically mixed 10–11-year-old children (13 boys and 12 girls). Both class teachers were female.

In the third-year class, the children were seated around six groups of tables. Three of the groups of tables were occupied solely by girls, the other three by boys. During the intervention phase of the study, the boys and girls were mixed so that boys and girls were now sitting next to each other. In the fourth-year class, the children were seated at conventional double desks, not tables. The desks were arranged in three rows and, with the exception of one boy who sat on his own, all of the children usually sat next to a member of the opposite sex. During the intervention period, girls and boys in each row changed places so that they were now sitting by a member of the same sex.

A version of the OPTIC schedule was again used to record classroom behaviour. For this study, the schedule was amended to differentiate between boys and girls in the various behaviour categories. An ABA or reversal design was employed. Data were collected over a two week baseline period, followed by a two-week intervention phase, then a reversal allowing the collection of two more weeks of baseline data. The alteration of seating arrangement for boys and girls in both classes took place during phase 2. All observations, in both the rows classrooms and the groups classrooms were taken during maths and English lessons throughout the three phases of the study.

During the baseline phase, mean on-task behaviour was 75% for the class seated in groups. When a mixed-sex seating arrangement was employed, the mean on-task level rose to 92%. The return to single-sex seating resulted in a lower mean on-task level of 67%. Comparison of pupil on-task behaviour for the boys and the girls showed clearly that both sexes were similarly affected by changes in seating arrangement. The figures for pupils' disruptive behaviour also showed movements in the expected direction over the three phases. During the baseline phase the mean number of disruptions was 22, during intervention the figure was 11 and for the return to baseline phase, 41. Again, both boys' and girls' disruptive behaviours were affected by the changes of seating arrangement. Over all three experimental phases, the boys were observed to be more disruptive than the girls.

The results for on-task behaviour in the class seated in rows showed that during the baseline phase, when a mixed-sex seating arrangement was in force, the mean on-task level was 90%. During the intervention phase, when the children changed to a single-sex seating arrangement, the mean on-task level fell to 76%. The return to baseline with normal mixed-sex seating arrangements resulted in an increased mean on-task level of 89%. The results for boys and girls separately were again very similar. The means for pupil disruption were 10 during baseline, 19 during intervention and for the return to baseline phase, 8. Thus, over the three phases the movement was in the expected direction for both on-task behaviour and rate of disruptions.

These results clearly showed that on-task behaviour in the class seated in rows decreased when the children of the same sex sat together, whereas in the class seated in groups, on-task behaviour increased when the normal same-sex seating was changed in favour of mixed-sex grouping. Thus, in these two classes with differing furniture configurations, the conclusion to be drawn is that mixed-sex seating produces the highest pupil on-task levels. Similarly, disruptive behaviour in both classes was at its lowest when boys and girls sat together. What also emerged clearly from the results was that the children with the lowest on-task study levels were the most positively affected by the change from mixed to same-sex seating.

What the results of this study do not show is whether the rises in on-task levels were accompanied by increases in the quantity and quality of academic work produced. Some tentative evidence for this is provided in another study carried out by one of our Master's degree students (Wigley) who demonstrated similar effects with a class of older, secondary-aged pupils (Merrett and Wheldall, 1988a). This second, small-scale study was carried out in a large comprehensive school in the West Midlands. Subjects comprised a below-average third-year class of 27 pupils who were generally regarded as troublesome. Observations were completed during history lessons which were taught by a male history graduate of five years' experience. He commented that the pupils were 'not bad' but that he was 'always ready for an outbreak of trouble'.

The class was normally seated in rows of same-sex pairs. They were observed on three separate occasions during baseline, over a two-week period. During the intervention, pupils were told that they should not sit next to a member of the same sex, and they were again observed on three occasions. Finally, in the return to baseline phase, pupils were permitted to resume same sex seating and were observed three more times.

Percentage on-task estimates were calculated for each individual pupil and for the whole class. An attempt was also made to collect data on academic work output. In each lesson in each phase, the pupils were asked to underline the last word they had written after 12 minutes of writing time had elapsed. The number of words written by each individual in this time was counted and a class average was calculated.

Mean on-task behaviour during baseline (same-sex seating) was 76% and rose to 91% during the mixed-sex seating intervention. During the return to baseline phase mean on-task behaviour fell back to 83%. The results for boys and girls were very similar. Marginally more words were produced during mixed seating than during the (same-sex) baseline condition, and there was evidence for a bigger drop in production during the return to baseline phase. The effect was more pronounced for boys than for girls. The teacher's subjective judgement was that the work produced during the intervention was of a higher quality.

The results of this small-scale study, involving older secondary-aged pupils, confirmed the results of the earlier study with primary-aged pupils. Both boys and girls spent more time working when seated next to a member of the opposite sex than when seated next to a person of the same sex. Whether this would be true for pupils older than 13–14 years remains an empirical question. There is some evidence to suggest that the resulting on-task behaviour is accompanied by greater work output. Subsequent discussion with the pupils revealed that in general they felt that they concentrated less when seated next to (same-sex) friends, and that they felt that they had worked harder during the intervention phase.

Studies of pupil interaction by Boydell (1975) and Galton, Simon and Croll (1980) have reported that up to 80 per cent of pupil interactions in junior classrooms were between children of the same sex. It could be suggested, therefore, that in order to discourage interaction in lessons requiring the individual pupils to work on their own, it is only necessary to mix the sexes. Whether this is educationally desirable, however, is another matter, and one for teachers (and pupils) to decide for themselves. Again we would caution that seating should be structured according to the task-demands of the lesson. If it is essential that children work quietly and independently on set work, then this sort of strategy might be appropriate, but we should also be providing contexts and organizing lessons which encourage collaborative effort. To the extent that we should also be encouraging more interaction across genders, we might also consider organizing mixed seating, and setting tasks which require interaction and collaboration.

SEATING ARRANGEMENTS AND QUESTIONING

As we showed earlier, seating arrangements can also influence teacher behaviour. The maths teacher in the special school found it easier to praise and to refrain from reprimanding when his classes were seated in rows than when they were seated around tables. We have also found that where children sit in the classroom can also influence the number of questions the teacher asks them, as is shown in the following study, carried out in Papua, New Guinea (Moore and Glynn, 1984).

This study involved two classes in an urban primary school. The grade two class comprised 27 seven-year-old children and their female teacher, whereas the grade three class comprised 29 eight-year-old children and their male teacher. The children in both classes were seated in individual desks, arranged in five clusters in the grade two class and arranged in five rows in the grade three class. Data collected during a baseline phase, in which teacher questions to individual children were closely monitored, revealed that children seated in specific areas in each classroom received a disproportionately high or a disproportionately low number of teacher questions. The grade two class teacher addressed more questions to children sitting at the back than to those sitting at the front of the class, whereas the grade three class teacher addressed more questions to the children sitting in the middle rows. Next, individual children were systematically shifted into and out of specific areas.

In the grade two classroom, a multiple baseline design was employed with three pairs of children. Each pair consisted of a child from a high-question-rate zone and a child from a low-question-rate zone. Each pair of children was required to change places with each other at successive intervals. In the grade three class a similar procedure was followed except that the three pairs also subsequently swapped back to their original positions (a reversal or return to baseline phase). The results showed, overall, that five out of the six children who had previously been located in low-question-rate zones received more teacher questions following their move to a high-question-rate zone. Similarly, five of the six children who moved from high- to low-question-rate zones received fewer questions following their move.

This study suggests that where children sit in class can greatly influence the number of questions they are asked by the teacher. Clearly, this may have serious implications for the academic progress of some pupils. If the questions asked are designed to ascertain whether a particular concept has been understood, for example, then the monitoring of some children is going to be more effective than it is for others. If the teacher is using a sampling technique, whereby questions asked of a few serve to indicate the general level of understanding by the class as a whole, then this form of biased sampling will provide inaccurate feedback to the teacher. In short, the needs of some children will go unnoticed, especially if they remain in a low-question-rate zone for protracted periods.

The results of these studies on classroom seating arrangements, taken together, provide powerful evidence for the importance of the behavioural ecology of classrooms. The findings from such studies can be used to help teachers to work out strategies for more effective management of classroom social behaviour and to design more effective contexts for learning academic skills. By changing the ecological antecedents for certain behaviours, we may be able to bring about productive and worthwhile changes in children's behaviour without the need for more intrusive and possibly more time-consuming procedures based on continued teacher delivery of reinforcement. At the very least, the findings from this series of studies should cause us to question our current preoccupation with fixed classroom seating arrangements and to encourage us to experiment with seating so as to optimize the appropriate behaviours for different learning-tasks.

6

Managing Classroom Behaviour

'OK, that's enough . . . .settle down. . . .I said 'settle down' and I mean what I say, SETTLE DOWN. That's a bit better. Now then, carry on with – Barry, leave him alone. . . .Geoff give Barry his pen back, yes now, come on we haven't got all day. Happy now Barry? Good. Well, as I was saying, and I WON'T say it again – Sharron and Pauline talking again – get out your best books and carry on – what? Yes, of course. You've only got one best book, haven't you? Well get it out then. Stop sniggering, Darren. And WHEN you've found your best book, Sharron and Pauline, and you Simone, I don't expect that from you. . . .carry on with the work you did not finish yesterday. You didn't even start it, did you Malcolm? No. I'm not a bit surprised. . . . DARREN!. . . .'

Does this sound familiar? Many teachers find themselves forced into regular litanies of reprimands like this, sometimes several times every day. Note that a large number of the comments are not to do with the academic work set, as such. They are more to do with children's classroom behaviour. We made the point earlier that even the most carefully prepared lessons will have little effect if children spend most of their time and attention behaving in ways unrelated to the tasks set. Teachers often refer to this as 'messing about'.

But, of course, what constitutes 'messing about' will vary from teacher to teacher and different teachers will have different tolerances for noise level and disruptive behaviour. They will also differ in terms of what they feel compelled to comment on. Some teachers seem to become obsessed with trivial matters such as dress (particularly school uniform) or length of hair, and these preoccupations are allowed to enter into their interactions with children and young people and interrupt the consideration of relevant academic matters. In our view, teachers would be well advised to reflect on their educational priorities and to determine which aspects of a pupil's style and behaviour are legitimately the concern of teachers and which are really a matter of personal preference. Neither of us has spiked hair and, in truth, do not usually find it attractive, but we fail to see what relevance hair style has to academic learning. To comment on such personal matters of taste would be considered impolite in most social contexts and it is difficult to see why some teachers feel that it is not only permissible but imperative that they do so. Such rude remarks and unsolicited comments about personal matters destroy the positive social context needed for effective learning.

We do acknowledge, however, that there are aspects of classroom social behaviour which teachers must concern themselves with. First, teachers are in the business of educating; sharing cultural information, experiences and values as well as skills and knowledge. So teachers should be concerned with helping children and young people to learn appropriate and socially acceptable ways of behaving in social situations, including classrooms. Second, social behaviours which prevent teachers getting on with their teaching and which prevent learning taking place are legitimate areas of concern. A positive, behavioural interactionist approach to teaching focuses on helping children and young people to learn to behave in the classroom in ways which will enhance academic learning. It is counter-productive to focus on problem behaviours. Certainly, continual nagging is not an effective way to improve pupils' classroom behaviour.

In the previous chapter we looked at the ways in which classroom seating can be a powerful ecological factor influencing social (and academic) behaviour. Getting the antecedents right is an important part of any classroom strategy for behaviour change. In this chapter we will examine classroom social behaviour, a source of conflict between many teachers and their classes. We will discuss ways in which a behavioural interactionist approach can be used to solve behaviour problems by encouraging more appropriate classroom behaviour. First, however, we will look briefly at just what behaviours teachers do find troublesome and report some of our findings on this topic.

CLASSROOM BEHAVIOUR PROBLEMS

Disruptive behaviour in the classroom is widely acknowledged as being one of the major problems facing many teachers. Children with behaviour problems are a common type of referral to educational psychologists. Nor are such problems confined to secondary schools as the results of our several surveys of both primary- and secondary-school teachers have shown (Merrett and Wheldall, 1974, 1987b; Wheldall and Merrett, 1988; Houghton, Wheldall and Merrett, 1988). In this section, we review the results from our main primary-school survey and our main secondary school survey which enquired into the frequency and kinds of troublesome behaviour experienced by teachers in their classrooms.

The primary survey (Wheldall and Merrett, 1988) constituted a 25% random sample (32 schools) of the infant, junior and junior/ infant schools in a West Midlands education authority in the UK. Sufficient survey forms were sent to each of these schools for each full-time class teacher to complete the questionnaire. Replies were received from all 32 schools resulting in a very high return rate of 93%, with 198 teachers responding.

Half of the sample (51%) responded affirmatively to our first question, 'Do you think that you spend more time on problems of order and control than you ought?' with the same percentage of affirmative response from men and women. The average class size was 27, of whom 4.3 children, on average, were regarded by their teachers as troublesome. Three of these were boys. Asked to identify the two most troublesome children in their class, 76% of the teachers identified a boy as the most troublesome and 77% of the teachers identified a boy as the second most troublesome. This supports the anecdotal view that boys do tend to be regarded as more troublesome than girls.

What was it that these children did that was so troublesome? It was the type and frequency of troublesome behaviours in which we were particularly interested. We offered ten alternative behaviour categories based on information from our pilot inquiries. When asked to pick out the most troublesome behaviour, 46% of teachers cited 'talking out of turn' (TOOT), which was defined as calling out to the teacher when not called upon, chattering about non-work-related matters, and making unwanted comments and remarks. This was followed by 'hindering other children' (HOC), chosen by 25% of teachers. None of the other categories was chosen by more than 10% of teachers. This was confirmed by the results for the second most troublesome behaviour, in which 31% opted for HOC and 17% for TOOT. The findings for the most *frequent* troublesome behaviours gave a very similar picture and when we went on to ask about the troublesome behaviours of individual children who were cited as being troublesome, again we got the same response, TOOT followed by HOC. The category 'physical aggression' was cited by fewer than 1% as being most troublesome and this placed the category tenth (last) in rank order.

We subsequently carried out a survey of the opinions of secondary-school teachers in the West Midlands (Houghton, Wheldall and Merrett, 1988) using a very similar questionnaire. The survey was based upon a random sample of about 30% of the secondary schools in the same West Midlands district as before. Replies were received from all six schools approached, yielding a return of 62%. Of the 251 secondary teachers responding, 55% admitted to spending more time on problems of order and control than they ought. Once again TOOT (50%) and HOC (17%) were readily identified as by far the most frequent and troublesome classroom behaviours. Physical violence and verbal abuse were very rarely cited. As at the primary level, boys were again identified as the most troublesome pupils by the majority of teachers.

What may we conclude from these results? We would be safe in assuming that the classroom behaviour problems experienced by most primary- and secondary-school teachers are similar. TOOT and HOC appear to be the two misbehaviours which teachers generally identify as causing them the most trouble and as occurring most often. This is not to say that serious incidents do not occur occasionally in some schools, but they are certainly not as frequent as the media would have us believe. Physical violence appears to be a problem encountered (thankfully) by relatively few teachers; but many, if not most, teachers have their job made more difficult by the petty misbehaviours which we have identified.

Most teachers would agree that TOOT and HOC are not particularly serious misbehaviours, in the sense that they are hardly crimes; but they are irritating, time-wasting, exhausting and stressful. The good news is that these sorts of classroom problem behaviours have been shown to be particularly amenable to resolution by behavioural methods, at both primary and secondary levels, as we will show in the rest of this chapter.

CLASSROOM PROCEDURES FOR CHANGING BEHAVIOUR

So far in this book, we have discussed the use of reinforcement only in fairly general terms. It is now appropriate to consider in more detail examples of the careful use of reinforcement to increase appropriate classroom behaviours. A behavioural approach can take many forms and is appropriate for all ages and stages, from pre-school (see, for example, Wheldall and Wheldall, 1981) to higher education (Pickthorne and Wheldall, 1982). The ways in which a behavioural approach is put into practice vary from situation to situation. Demonstrations of the effectiveness of behavioural interventions also differ in terms of the precision with which they are carried out and evaluated. The rigorous designs beloved of behavioural researchers cut less ice with practical teachers, for whom simple 'suck it and see' methods are more convincing. Both forms of demonstration study are necessary. Let us begin with a study which is little more than an anecdote but which, nevertheless, proved a very rewarding lesson for the teacher, nursery assistant and parents involved.

A Simple, Individual Case Study

A few years ago, in the nursery class in the Centre for Child Study at the University of Birmingham, the two staff were concerned about a four-year-old boy. Gavin came from a caring professional family, but in comparison with the other children in the nursery, he seemed to our staff to be 'rather immature'. Pressed to be specific, the nursery teacher and nursery assistant described how he very rarely played with the other children, never initiated interactions and, in fact, did not seem to do very much for himself at all. He behaved, they said, in some ways more like a two-year-old than a four year old and was 'babied' by his parents.

Our casual observations confirmed the worries of the nursery staff. Gavin spent most of his time standing on the fringe of the nursery action watching or day-dreaming, with his thumb in his mouth. Both nursery class staff employed positive methods and were 'au fait' with our behavioural approach, but they reported that straight praise seemed to have little effect on Gavin. It certainly did not seem to encourage him to participate more. We suggested that a more powerful reward might be necessary in the form of tokens. The usual sort of star chart is not appropriate for pre-school children, and so a long snake, divided up into a number of sections, was drawn for him on cardboard. It was explained to Gavin that whenever he completed an activity, he would be allowed to colour in one of the segments of his snake. When his snake was complete he would receive a reward, a small model tractor which he was very keen to have.

It is only fair to add that the nursery-class staff were not, at this stage, totally convinced that this scheme would work for Gavin. Nevertheless, they enthusiastically put the scheme into operation and began by suggesting activities to him; for example, painting a picture or building a Lego model. Gavin, to his credit, responded to these suggestions and consequently earned his points and the right to colour succeeding segments of the snake. Later on, the nursery-class staff asked him what he wanted to do next, as a prompt, and he continued to be rewarded every time he completed an activity. After some time, he gradually began to initiate activities himself, pausing only to tell the staff that he had finished and to colour another segment. In our view, children's successful initiation of activities and interactions is an important sign of independent learning.

Gavin's progress was remarkable and by the end of the first week he had completed his snake and was delighted to receive his reward. Another snake programme was immediately initiated, at Gavin's request. No formal data were collected apart from the implicit recording of completed activities in the colouring-in of the snake. This visual record of progress confirmed informal observations of Gavin's increased activity level. Instead of almost literally 'doing nothing', Gavin was now clearly seen to be engaging in several different activities every morning, to the satisfaction of the nursery-class staff. We believe that the snake chart made Gavin more aware of his growing success. Initially, praise alone may not have been reinforcing for Gavin in this context. Excessive 'babying' by Gavin's parents may have restricted his opportunities to learn to initiate interactions. Over time, in association with the snake chart providing non-verbal reinforcement for Gavin's own attempts to take control, praise may have become more effective.

An unplanned bonus for the nursery-class staff came from Gavin's parents, who had been told about the programme and who had been encouraged to praise Gavin for his progress on the snake. Shortly after the programme began they reported improvements in his behaviour at home. These improvements at home further support the notion that Gavin was assuming more control over his own behaviour and becoming less dependent on his teachers. He rapidly began to change from being a passive child with little interest in his world to a far more active individual with a lively curiosity. As Gavin was approaching the age to begin formal schooling, these were important developments.

The informal report above illustrates how in some situations formal data collection is not always essential. The changes were sufficiently large and obvious to impress both nursery-class staff and parents. In the following studies, however, more formal and objective data collection procedures were employed in carefully designed experiments. These experimental studies further demonstrate the effectiveness of behavioural interventions with other classes of children, of different ages.

A Touch of Reinforcement

In the previous example, non-verbal reinforcement in the form of completed coloured segments on the snake chart proved effective with Gavin where praise alone did not. Two further studies are now discussed which also involve non-verbal reinforcement, this time in the form of teacher touch (Wheldall, Bevan and Shortall, 1986). The aim of our first study was to examine the effect of positive contingent teacher touch on the classroom behaviour of infant-class children. We wanted to know whether reducing the use of non-contingent touch behaviour and increasing the use of positive contingent touch behaviour to accompany praise by teachers would lead to children's on-task behaviour increasing and their disruptive behaviour decreasing. The study was carried out in two infant classes in a small primary school in the West Midlands, where about 65% of the children came from Asian-immigrant home backgrounds. We chose infant classes since teachers of younger children (five- to six-year olds) were more likely to employ touch as part of their natural teaching style. Both teachers were female and experienced.

Each teacher and her class were observed for ten 30-minute sessions, using an early version of the OPTIC schedule adapted to include teacher touch behaviour. Touch was defined as 'the teacher's hand, or part of the hand, and/or arm in contact with the child's body.' Following the baseline sessions, both teachers were instructed to touch children only when they praised them for appropriate academic and/or social behaviour and not to touch children for other purposes including 'instruction' or 're-direction' (both of which categories were explained to teachers). It was emphasized that no deliberate increase of praise was required or to be attempted. Both teachers were again observed, as before, for a further ten sessions. In both classes, when teachers touched children together with praising them, on-task behaviour rose by over 15%, from around 75% to 90%, and disruptions fell from about ten or eleven per session to only two or three instances. Both teachers substantially increased their contingent use of touch (mainly linked to approval for academic behaviour) and decreased their use of non-contingent touch.

The second study was carried out to replicate the first but using a more rigorous, multiple baseline design with two further infant classes. The procedure was introduced into the second class a week after being introduced into the first class. This study was carried out in a similar infant school in the West Midlands, with 95% of the children coming from Asian backgrounds. Both teachers were again female and experienced. Data on on-task behaviour and teacher behaviours were collected for 15minutes each day for three weeks. Baseline data collection began on the same day for both classes, but whereas this consisted of only one week (five sessions) in class 1 prior to intervention, in class 2 the baseline condition was extended to two weeks (ten sessions) prior to intervention. Data collection continued for a further two weeks following intervention in class 1 and for one further week in class 2, according to the multiple baseline design. For both classes the intervention consisted of instructing the teachers to touch the children only when they were praising them and not to attempt to increase rate of praise. For class 1 on-task behaviour rose from nearly 40% to nearly 70%, and for class 2 from 50% to 65%, when teacher touch was paired with praise. Both teachers were successful in reducing their overall use of non-contingent touch following the intervention, and increased their contingent use of touch (i.e. accompanying approval) substantially.

These two studies, involving four teachers, provide evidence for the effectiveness of teacher touch as a reinforcer for appropriate classroom behaviour, when it accompanies praise. In all four cases, mean class on-task behaviour increased substantially following the inclusion of touch, by an average of 20%, and, where measured, rates of disruptive behaviour fell markedly. In other words, across the four different studies, children spent about a third again as much time working compared with baseline levels. Given four replications of the effect, this is reasonably strong evidence for the effectiveness of teacher touch combined with praise as a powerful reinforcer of young children's classroom behaviour.

By using contingent, positive touch in association with praise, teachers will also be helping children to experience the reinforcing effects of teacher praise. Verbal praise may not be very meaningful to some young children, especially those from home backgrounds where the first language is not English, but accompanied by positive, contingent teacher touch, its meaning is clear. Touch is also a naturally occurring reinforcer in human social interaction, and hence may be preferable to contrived reinforcers, such as the snake chart in the earlier study. This is not to say that there is not a place for contrived reinforcers, as a first step with children who do not respond to less intrusive reinforcers, but touch, and later praise alone, will prepare a child better for the 'real world'. The use of such naturally occurring reinforcers is also more likely to lead to the learned behaviours generalizing to other settings, settings which may not permit the use of contrived reinforcers.

Rules, Praise and Ignoring

The ways of managing behaviour in an unruly classroom are many and various, but the key principle is basically: praise the good, and try to ignore the bad. One of the most widely used techniques is known as RPI or 'rules, praise and ignoring'. RPI was originally devised in the United States by Madsen, Becker and Thomas (1968) and has subsequently been extensively employed as a general classroom management procedure. In brief, it requires the teacher to negotiate (ideally) a set of three or four short, positively phrased rules covering acceptable classroom behaviours. These often take the form of simple declarations of intent such as: 'We try to get on with our work quietly' or 'We put up our hands when we want to ask a question.'

It is important that these rules are negotiated or at least discussed with and justified to the children to whom they will apply. This process is important because it amounts to sharing some of the control over classroom behaviour with the children themselves. If they can propose and discuss the application of new rules and participate in the exact formulation of rules, it is more likely that they will learn something of how to change their own behaviour and will be less likely to challenge the rules. The newly negotiated rules are then written up boldly and displayed. Our own experience is that primary classes in particular respond with enthusiasm to this procedure, the members of one class spontaneously signing their names to the rule sheet when it was pinned to the wall! Thinking in terms of our ABC model, it will be apparent that the rules component of RPI is being explicitly employed as a functional antecedent for behaviour. Rules act, in fact, as a form of 'prompt' and teachers operating RPI are encouraged to draw attention to the rules regularly, preferably when pupils are clearly keeping the rules, but not when they are being infringed.

Praise and ignoring refer to the consequence aspects of the RPI procedure. Quite simply, teachers are required to praise pupils for keeping the rules ('catch the children being good') and to ignore infractions of the rules. Praise may be addressed to the whole class or to individuals, but should refer specifically to their behaviour in keeping the rules. Ignoring is often more difficult for teachers and is frequently misunderstood. It refers only to the behaviours governed by the rules and does not mean that teachers should not intervene if a fight breaks out or if pupils are about to do something dangerous. The idea is to avoid responding to rule-related misbehaviours. Doing this may prove counter-productive if some of the children involved find any form of teacher attention reinforcing. A high rate of teacher attention to rule-breaking also undermines the overall positive context of teacher–child interaction.

It must be emphasized that ignoring (without rules and praise) has been shown to be ineffective. As a technique on its own, ignoring has certainly been 'over-sold' to teachers. 'Ignore it and it will go away', the sloppy advice sometimes given to teachers by those with a superficial knowledge of the behavioural approach, is nonsense to a teacher who knows he or she cannot permit certain behaviour excesses to continue without intervention. Such teachers recognize that their attention to or ignoring of certain behaviours like showing off to peers would be overwhelmed by the strength of peer approval or even just peer attention to these behaviours. An unsuccessful or unpopular child who gains acceptance or a laugh from his peers for fooling about is unlikely to be much affected by teacher ignoring. The technique of ignoring is at least partly predicated upon the assumption that even negative teacher attention may be rewarding; the hard truth is that teacher response may be irrelevant in the face of frequent and powerful peer attention. This may be particularly true for adolescents.

Becker, Madsen, Arnold and Thomas (1967) and Madsen, Becker and Thomas (1968) carried out what are now regarded as classic studies in classroom behaviour management, comparing various combinations of these three basic procedures. The first condition, rules only, had little effect in reducing undesirable behaviour. The results were still inconsistent when 'ignoring' was added. But the third combination, in which praise was added to 'rules' and 'ignoring', was shown to be a highly effective procedure for maintaining classroom control. They concluded that 'praise for appropriate behaviour was probably the essential teacher behaviour in achieving effective classroom management' (Madsen Becker and Thomas, 1968).

A subsequent experiment by Thomas, Becker and Armstrong (1968) showed how 'good' teachers who normally maintain a well ordered classroom by ignoring inappropriate behaviours and by consistently reinforcing appropriate behaviours can, by altering these contingencies, produce dramatic deterioration in classroom behaviour. In one study, disruptive behaviour was raised from the usual low level of around 8–9% to over 40% accompanied by an appreciable rise in noise level. This was 'achieved' by the teacher frequently expressing disapproval for inappropriate behaviours. Thus it has been shown experimentally that while reinforcing (by expressing approval of) desirable behaviours leads to increased good behaviour, attending to inappropriate behaviour, even by expressing disapproval, may increase the very behaviours it is attempting to reduce. It has similarly been shown that increasing the number of 'sit down' commands actually increases the amount of out-of-seat behaviour, while praising for in seat behaviour reduces out-of-seat behaviour.

In one of our early studies demonstrating effective classroom behaviour management (Merrett and Wheldall, 1978), we attempted to devise a positive approach which the children would find enjoyable. Rather than concentrating solely on trying to eliminate undesirable behaviours, which we know to be ineffective, we decided to concentrate on the behaviour the teacher was trying to bring about, i.e. the pupils getting on with their schoolwork. We tried to raise the frequency of what was, for this class, relatively infrequent behaviour. This approach was based on several previous studies which had also employed 'game' strategies.

The class teacher involved was young, relatively inexperienced, and was having trouble in controlling her class of 30 ten-to-eleven-year olds of below average achievement. Classroom seating was arranged around four tables and we decided to make use of this in our intervention strategy.

Initially we needed accurate information about the children's behaviour in the classroom. A cassette-tape was prepared to give a clear intermittent 'ping' on average once per minute. On hearing the sound the teacher would look at one of the four tables of children and note the behaviour of the target child for that table. The target child was chosen afresh for each observation session on a random basis. All children were observed during the study. Every time she heard the 'ping' the teacher was instructed to glance at a schedule to see which table was next and to record the behaviour of the target child. Baseline data were collected over several weeks. These data comprised observations made of children's behaviour before the game procedure was introduced. By averaging over sessions we calculated that the children were on-task, i.e. quietly getting on with their work, only 44% of the time. The teacher was then given some basic instruction in the behavioural approach and the game strategy was suggested to her. She readily agreed to implement this.

Briefly, the children were told the rules of a 'game' which were:

1   we stay in our seats whilst working,
2   we get on quietly with our work,
3   we try not to interrupt.

While the game was in progress the cassette was switched on and every time the 'ping' sounded the teacher would look at one of the tables. If everyone on the table was keeping the rules, then each child on the table scored a point. (The children were assured that all tables would get equal turns but that the order would be random.) Each time a point was given it was accompanied by praise. This procedure lasted for five weeks, when an amendment was introduced. Points were now awarded on only 50% of the 'pings', again on a random basis. The 'pings' continued to serve as a signal for the teacher to observe and record the behaviour of the target children as well as a signal for reinforcement. This procedure therefore focuses as much on changing teacher behaviour as it does on changing child behaviour.

The results were remarkable and immediate. From the baseline on-task behaviour of only 44%, on-task behaviour rose to 77% following the intervention (the introduction of the game). Moreover, when the amendment to the schedule of reinforcement was made the on-task behaviour rose even higher to between 80 and 100%. Interestingly the quality of 'off-task' behaviour also changed. Whereas before the intervention disruptiveness mainly comprised loud talking and movement around the room, after intervention it consisted mainly of passive inattention, day-dreaming and watching other children.

A purely subjective estimate of the classroom after the intervention was of great improvement in terms of orderliness and quiet during classroom work periods. An attempt was also made to measure academic output both before and after intervention. For example, samples of written work taken from the class during the collection of baseline data showed a mean output of approximately five written words per minute. During one of the first intervention sessions this had improved to a mean of approximately 13 written words. The number of spelling errors, despite the increase in output, scarcely altered.

The teacher used the term 'harrowing' to describe her problems with class control in her first (probationary) year. Recording baseline data had proved 'tedious and time-consuming' at first, but she thought that it became easier and less distracting with practice. She said she 'felt silly' about putting up the wall chart of rules, but she agreed that the effect of the intervention was immediate and powerful. Some of the children were also asked their opinion of the game. Of the 13 who responded, 12 were approving. All of those approving commented that the quietness that prevailed enabled them to concentrate and get on with their work without interruption. What remains a mystery was the great reluctance of this teacher, who is not atypical, to use verbal reinforcers. It is difficult to understand why some teachers typically praise appropriate behaviours only infrequently, while continually commenting upon inappropriate behaviour.

This simple strategy, which we call 'playing the game', has proved to be very robust. Our findings have been replicated many times over by our students with many different age groups and in a variety of teaching contexts (Wheldall and Merrett, 1984). It does have limitations, however, not least the problem of generalizing the improved classroom behaviour to times and settings when the game is not in operation. It may also be intrusive and unsuitable for some lessons. Few teachers would want to use such a device often or for protracted periods. In spite of these reservations, however, it has repeatedly been shown to be a very effective means for gaining, or regaining, order with an unruly class, and is an excellent means of training teachers to 'catch children being good' and to increase their use of contingent praise. We have already observed that children's behaviour and teacher behaviour in the classroom are interactive.

Two of our earlier studies, carried out in New Zealand, employed a similar version of the 'rules, praise and ignoring' strategy coupled with a self-management procedure to assist children to learn to take responsibility for their own classroom behaviour. When an intermittent 'ping' sounded at varying intervals on a tape-recorder, children were asked to decide whether or not they were on-task at that moment, and to mark a square on a reward card 'if the ping had caught them working'. In the first study (Glynn, Thomas and Shee, 1973) five- and six- year-old children found no difficulty in operating this procedure and in maintaining the high level of their own on-task behaviour achieved by the RPI strategy. In the second study (Glynn and Thomas, 1974), a class of seven- and eight-year-old children were introduced directly to the self-management procedure without prior experience of the RPI strategy. These children at first experienced some difficulty in operating the procedure. This was because their teacher kept changing his mind about whether the children should be 'working quietly' at their tasks or whether they should 'stop, look and listen' while he discussed examples of inappropriate classroom behaviour as they occurred. He alternated his demands from 'work quietly' to 'stop, look and listen' so often that when a 'ping' occurred the children were confused as to what they were supposed to be doing to qualify for being on-task at that moment. We provided a 'cue card', one side showing 'stop, look and listen' lettered in red, and the other side showing 'work quietly' lettered in green. We asked the teacher to display the cue card on a ledge and to turn it over every time he changed his instruction. Following the correct use of this cue card by the teacher, children in this class also operated the self-management procedure successfully. The observed level of on-task behaviour in the classroom increased markedly when the cue card component was added to the self-management procedure. In both of these studies, therefore, clearly specified rules combined with a simple self-management procedure established a context in which young children learned to take the major share of control over their own behaviour in the classroom.

WILL IT WORK IN SECONDARY SCHOOLS?

A common reaction to reports of studies such as those described above is that such an approach would only work with young children. And, in fact, relatively few of the many studies reporting behavioural interventions in schools refer to secondary schools, as Merrett's (1981) review makes clear. Many teachers are sceptical of success in secondary settings, believing that at best it would necessitate highly complex and time-consuming procedures. We have now carried out a number of studies, however, which demonstrate the effectiveness of behavioural approaches to classroom management with classes of older, secondary-school children. The first study to be reported evolved as a demonstration that effective behaviour management could be achieved using only 'light' behavioural procedures (Wheldall and Austin, 1980).

This study took place in a large comprehensive school in a disadvantaged urban area of the West Midlands and involved a difficult class of 25 fourteen-year olds from the lowest three of ten 'streams'. All of the teachers involved with this class admitted difficulties privately but were reluctant to admit them publicly. The headmaster, who taught the class remedial maths for five lessons per week, volunteered to take part. He was an impressive teacher who rarely shouted and who used relatively high rates of praise. The class appeared to like and respect him but our 11 days of baseline observation showed that they were on-task only 55% of the time. Many of the students were often off-task because they had finished the set work (usually a set of 'sums' or other maths problems put up on the board) and did not know what to do next. Others had not finished but were being disturbed by those who had. We suggested that a few more problems be put up on the board for the quicker children to get on with while the slower ones caught up. (This provided an antecedent for continued on-task behaviour.)

The headmaster agreed and the observations for the next seven lessons showed on-task behaviour improved by nearly 15% to an average of around 70%. We decided that this could be improved still further. A comparison was made between a 'light' strategy of using only a simple 'rules, praise and ignore' procedure and a 'heavier' alternative, whereby points could be earned which gained free time. The two strategies were compared using an alternating-conditions research design. The simple 'rules, praise and ignoring' procedure alternated daily with a 'points plus free time' strategy. This strategy was a group contingency whereby the whole class could earn one minute's free time each time they were all on-task when a timer sounded at intermittent intervals. Free time was taken during the Friday afternoon lesson.

The headmaster agreed to these procedures and the results were dramatic. The data clearly showed further improvement in on-task behaviour, to over 80% with the 'rules, praise and ignoring' strategy and to over 90% during the 'points plus free time' sessions. Over time both strategies yielded rates of around 95% 'on-task'. The study thus provided a clear demonstration of successful implementation of behavioural approaches in a secondary school, and also demonstrated the power of simple procedures such as contingent praise combined with altering an antecedent event (making sure additional work was available for those who finished early).

In another study we again used 'rules, praise and ignoring' but this time with pupils in four secondary home-economics classes in a school in the West Midlands (Wheldall and Merrett, 1987a). In this study the rules were not negotiated since, for the purposes of the experiment, it was important that exactly the same conditions obtained in all of the experimental classes. (We advocate that rules should usually be negotiated with a class to suit the particular circumstances of that class.) The rules used in this study, which could be a little more complicated with these older pupils, were as follows:

1 We try to work quietly and put up our hands when we need help.
2 We listen carefully to instructions and read the board and our recipe sheets carefully.
3 We try to work tidily in our units and share the jobs when clearing away.
4 We get on with our cooking without disturbing others.

In view of the points made earlier about rules, praise and ignoring, and especially since the procedures were employed in home economics practical (cookery) lessons in this study, teacher reprimands for potentially dangerous behaviour were not precluded. Teachers were, however, instructed to ignore rule infringements wherever possible and to concentrate on praising rule-keeping and 'on-task' behaviours. The teachers were also asked to make a general evaluative summary statement at the end of each lesson concerning their class's behaviour during that lesson. For example, 'You have all worked much harder today than last week: let's see if you can do even better next week.'

The study involved four second-year classes of 20 to 30 twelve- and thirteen-year-old boys and girls and their three experienced teachers (one teacher taught two classes). All four classes had gained a reputation for noisiness, untidiness and not listening. The aims of the study were to demonstrate that simple behavioural methods could be used effectively in home-economics practical lessons to encourage more attention to the task in hand and, especially, to reduce the excessive noise levels commonly experienced in such practical classes. To this end, all four classes were systematically observed for 30 minutes during the practical component of their weekly lesson over an eight-week period. These observations were completed by our student who had been carefully trained to use the OPTIC classroom behaviour observation schedule. In addition, the observer was also able to obtain objective measures of noise level by using a decibel meter.

In order to demonstrate the effectiveness of the procedures clearly and rigorously, a multiple baseline design was employed. 'Rules, praise and ignoring' was introduced successively at two-week intervals with the four classes. All classes were observed operating normally for the first two weeks and then 'rules, praise and ignoring' was introduced in the first class. Two weeks later it was also introduced into the second class and after a further two weeks into the third class. The fourth class remained under baseline conditions throughout. The multiple baseline design was employed to show how the intervention consistently and unequivocally exerts its effect upon behaviour, class by class.

In each of the three experimental classes average on-task behaviour rose following the introduction of the intervention; in the first class from 78% to 83%; more markedly in the second class from around 75% to 89%; and in the third class from about 75% to 85%. In the fourth class, of course, on-task behaviour averaged about 83% throughout, since no 'rules, praise and ignoring' was attempted with this (control) class.

The effects of the strategy were shown even more clearly on noise level. Again in each of the three experimental classes noise level was shown to fall markedly following the introduction of 'rules, praise and ignoring'; in the first class from an average of around 66db to 62db; in the second class from 68db to 63db; and in the third class from 69db to 61db. In the fourth (control) class noise level remained constant at around 63db. These reductions in noise level were substantial and clearly noticeable.

In all of the studies reported so far we have described strategies based on praise and reward. We have commented that teacher nagging is unlikely to be effective and should be reduced, if not eliminated. But this is not to say that there is no place for the occasional use of discreet reprimands. In one of our recent studies (Houghton, Wheldall, Jukes and Sharpe, 1988), we compared two behaviour management procedures in four secondary-school classes, using a multiple baseline design. Two of the four teachers taking part in the study were found to use high rates of loud reprimand and low rates of praise with their classes. Following baseline observations, these two teachers were asked to limit their use of reprimands to ten or fewer. They were also asked to move closer to the pupil being reprimanded, to make eye-contact and to state quietly but firmly exactly what was being disapproved of. In both classes on-task behaviour increased by around 15% and rose a further 10% when a second strategy – private, specific praising – was also introduced.

The other two teachers, who used few reprimands and few praise statements during baseline, were initially asked to give 20 private, specific praise statements per lesson. On-task behaviour rose by about

12% as a result and increased by a further 6 or 7% when the two teachers were also asked to employ up to five private reprimands per lesson. Taken together, the results for the four teachers suggest that there is a role for reprimands if used sparingly, specifically and privately and in a positive context overall.

What Do Adolescent Pupils Find Reinforcing?

These studies provide evidence of the effectiveness of behavioural methods, and they add further to the body of experimental data confirming that the behavioural approach is equally applicable to older, secondary aged pupils as to younger children. One of the legitimate reservations about using behavioural methods with older children, however, is the need for more powerful back-up reinforcers with more difficult or poorly motivated pupils. The disenchanted, potentially troublesome teenage pupil is less likely to find the traditional privilege of 'feeding the guinea pig' rewarding and so it is important to ask, 'What do secondary aged pupils find reinforcing?'

We recently carried out a study on this topic (Sharpe, Wheldall and Merrett, 1987) following up earlier work carried out with Australian adolescents (Sharpe, 1986). We surveyed the attitudes and opinions of nearly 400 secondary pupils aged 12 to 16 years attending two comprehensive schools in the West Midlands. A 'Praise and Rewards Attitude Questionnaire' (PRAQ) inquired into pupils' preferences for various types of reward for both academic and social behaviour. We found that most British secondary pupils do perceive rewards and praise as appropriate outcomes for both academic and social behaviour, although older pupils tend to regard them as more appropriate for academic behaviour alone. Our results also showed that when offered a choice of six alternative rewards (sweets, free time, no reward, praise, points or a positive letter home), free time and a positive letter home were most highly regarded.

Free time is perhaps predictable as a reinforcer. It is relatively easily arranged and has certainly been shown to be effective, as the study carried out in the secondary maths class (described above) clearly showed. Free time is an effective reinforcer because the complex timetabling in large secondary schools affords pupils surprisingly few opportunities just to enjoy each other's company in a relaxed, unstructured context. For many pupils, school is the only place where they can regularly interact with the peer group beyond their immediate neighbourhood. Secondary schools do not often utilize this powerful reinforcer available to them.

A positive letter home was much less predictable as a reinforcer and is hardly ever employed in secondary schools. A letter home is normally only used to convey disapproval of social or academic behaviour. Its use in a positive form as a reward needs to be explored experimentally but it is certainly a 'cheap' option which can readily be arranged. It should be noted that free time and a positive letter were the favoured choices of pupils for both social and academic behaviour. People of all ages respond to a range of intrinsic and extrinsic reinforcers. Secondary-school pupils are no exception and respond favourably to various forms of praise and reward which are available for use by the teacher. A subsequent study replicated and extended these findings by asking, in addition, what punishments and sanctions secondary pupils considered to be effective, this time with nearly 900 pupils (Houghton, Merrett and Wheldall, 1988). Again, free time and a letter home were regarded as effective rewards for both academic and social behaviours while the most effective punishments were perceived to be 'a letter home complaining about you' and 'being put on report'. There appears to be a serious mismatch betwen the punishments and sanctions most used by teachers (like telling off and sending out) and those regarded as effective by their pupils. On the other hand, some actions which are regarded as effective by pupils are seldom, if ever, used by teachers. Nevertheless, and perhaps surprisingly, the vast majority of pupils who were asked, claimed to value their teachers' opinions about their work and their conduct more highly than that of their peers.

We then went on to ask schools about the systems of sanction and reward they employed to regulate pupil behaviour (Merrett, Wilkins, Houghton and Wheldall, 1988). As we noted in chapter 4, the most common way teachers have of dealing with disruptive behaviour is to reprimand offending pupils, rather than to encourage more appropriate classroom behaviour. A similar pattern is reflected in the systems schools employ to regulate pupils' behaviour. We were interested to know more about the rules and sanctions systems currently employed in secondary schools and so we carried out a survey, using structured interviews with head teachers or their nominees, involving all of the secondary schools (24 in number) in a local education authority in the West Midlands. The structured interview schedule was designed to obtain information about the nature and form of the rules in each school and then to explore the sanction and reward system devised to uphold them.

Most schools (21) had well-defined rule systems, usually written down, which were made available to all pupils (and their parents) when they began to attend the school. These rules usually formed part of an introductory booklet. In 12 schools the rules had been formulated within the last five years but in some, rules dated from 14 and 17 years previously and had not been reviewed in the interim. Most schools used a hierarchy of sanctions to ensure that the pupils kept these rules which extend from telling off, lines or detention to writing to parents and involving them in the task of seeing that pupils conform. As a last resort, all schools had the sanctions of suspension or expulsion which involve outside authorities as well.

Most of the rules, as in society at large, were framed in negative terms ('Thou shalt not'), and sanctions are applied to those who disobey the eleventh commandment and allow themselves to be caught. Prohibitive rules such as these serve to define what will not be tolerated, but give no indication of alternative, acceptable behaviours. Another characteristic of this system, which most teachers recognize, is that the sanctions apply to only a small minority of the pupil population. The same names appear again and again in the punishment book.

Very few schools (only one in the present survey) involve pupils in helping to frame the rules or even to approve them once decided upon, and even fewer attempt to phrase the rules positively. Again, few schools had any incentive system for rewarding pupils who keep the rules and so conform well to the mores of the school society. Most schools have ways of rewarding children who achieve high standards in certain fields such as physical education, music and so on. However, apart from certificates for passing examinations, which are long term and far beyond the reach of a large number of pupils, there is little by way of reward or encouragement for the majority, and nothing to encourage appropriate behaviour in any.

To sum up, our research shows that teachers can be positive, encouraging and supportive of pupils' academic efforts, but when it comes to their classroom behaviour the emphasis appears to be almost overwhelmingly negative. The continual litany of reprimands we hear on entering some secondary classes is almost always an attempt to deal with disruptive classroom behaviours. Very rarely are attempts made to encourage more appropriate forms of classroom behaviour. The focus is on detecting and dealing with inappropriate behaviour rather than recognizing and rewarding appropriate behaviour. Similarly, the systems which schools develop for maintaining discipline are structured so as to punish transgressions rather than to encourage more responsible behaviour. Negatively-phrased, prohibitive rules are determined and imposed by senior staff, with little consultation with junior staff let alone pupils, and are not always regularly reviewed to keep pace with rapidly changing societal norms and values.

ON-TASK BEHAVIOUR AND ACADEMIC PERFORMANCE

In the timer game study carried out with the junior class, described earlier in this chapter (Merrett and Wheldall, 1978), the increase in on-task behaviour was clearly associated with academic gains. Similarly, increases in on-task behaviour resulting from changes in seating arrangements have also been associated with increased work output (see chapter 5). But reinforcing academic behaviour directly can also lead to increased on-task behaviour. Marholin and Steinman (1977) reviewed several studies which indicate that the amount of time a child spends on-task can be increased and the amount of disruption decreased by reinforcing academic achievement directly, without the need first or concurrently to reinforce on-task behaviour or other related social behaviours. They studied the on-task behaviour, number of maths problems attempted, and accuracy of eight fifth- and sixth-grade children. These behaviours were observed first under conditions where reinforcement was provided for on-task behaviour, and subsequently where reinforcement was provided for accuracy and rate of maths problems completed. The number of problems attempted increased, and the disruptive behaviour was reduced under conditions of reinforcement for accuracy and rate of maths problems completed. This was particularly noticeable during periods when the teacher was absent from the classroom.

Some of our research studies carried out in New Zealand also bear on this topic. One unpublished study showed that for four primary-school under-achievers in a class for disturbed children, reinforcement (tokens) contingent on their attending behaviour (being on-task) had little effect on their academic work output (written expression and maths). In contrast, reinforcement contingent upon academic work output greatly increased attending behaviour as well as improving academic output. In another study (Ballard and Glynn, 1975), we found that on-task behaviour for a class of grade three children was higher when they were writing stories and receiving reinforcement for components of writing than when they were writing stories under baseline conditions. A further study (Scriven and Glynn, 1983) involving under-achieving 14 and 15-year olds found that pupils' on-task behaviour steadily increased along with gains in rate of written expression resulting from a programme of explicit feedback to pupils. These studies will be reported in more detail in chapter 9.

The available evidence, then, suggests that we can increase attending (on-task) behaviour by reinforcing academic work completed or that, conversely, we can increase academic work completed by reinforcing attending behaviour. It should be noted, however, that the monitoring and reinforcing of attending behaviour can be carried out by children themselves, thereby greatly reducing the demands on the teacher. Again, several of our studies described earlier testify to the effectiveness of employing self-management procedures for improving on-task behaviour (Glynn, Thomas and Shee, 1973; Glynn and Thomas, 1974). However, while demonstrating clear gains in on-task behaviour,these studies did not include data on academic work completed. The children were performing a range of academic tasks which did not always lead to an observable permanent product, for example, playing word games or number games. The pupil self-managment procedures permitted the teacher to spend the majority of her time in one-to-one teaching and responding to initiations from individual children.

LEARNING BEHAVIOURAL SKILLS FOR MANAGING CLASSROOM BEHAVIOUR

In our experience, teachers who learn more about what a behavioural approach really entails often want to know how to learn behavioural teaching skills. Reading books and articles is a good way of finding out more about a subject but is not usually much help for learning new skills. This is as true for learning to teach as it is for learning to swim or drive a car or ride a bicycle. To learn new skills you need to practise, to monitor your performance and obtain feedback.

So how do we go about the business of helping teachers to learn behavioural skills to improve the effectiveness of their classroom management? At first, we hoped that a formal lecture programme about behavioural methods might prove helpful to teachers wanting to learn behavioural methods. We provided many references and mentioned many experiments but without much success. We found that telling teachers about behavioural methods improved their attitude towards, and increased their knowledge about, a behavioural approach but did little to change their behaviour, i.e. what they did in the classroom (Wheldall and Congreve, 1980; Merrett and Wheldall, 1982). Consequently, we learned the hard way that the emphasis has to be on skills-training: training teachers how to apply a behavioural approach in real teaching situations (and providing them with direct and individual feedback on their own performance) rather than just teaching them about behavioural principles.

The Behavioural Approach to Teaching Package, or BATPACK was developed at the Centre for Child Study at the University of Birmingham (Wheldall and Merrett, 1985; 1986; 1987b). Our aim was to develop a basic package for use in training practising primary- and middle-school teachers in a number of key behavioural skills. BATPACK was developed from the programme of experimental research into the behavioural approach to teaching carried out by our research team. The package has six distinguishing characteristics.

1   *BATPACK is skills based.* In BATPACK our primary aim is to change teacher behaviour by teaching new skills and techniques which can be implemented directly in the teacher's own classroom. By such skills we are referring, for example, to pin-pointing and observing specific child behaviours, positive rule-setting, effective praising and so on.

2   *BATPACK is school based.* BATPACK training is typically carried out in school with groups of about ten teachers, which would often include the whole of an infant, junior or middle school staff. It is essential that the idea is seen by the head teacher and his/her staff as something for the whole school which will be their system. This school-based training system provides support by instilling a team spirit whereby all members of the staff are working together, and gives them a common language for talking about children's behaviour problems.

3   *BATPACK is contract based.* We specify precisely, in advance and in practical terms, what is expected of the teachers and what the course tutor will provide. These points are then embodied in a contract which is agreed and signed by each course student and the tutor. The contract requires the tutor to start and finish all sessions on time and to provide all necessary materials. Course members contract to attend all sessions on time, to complete the work assignments between sessions, to try out the suggested techniques in class and to complete the evaluation sheets at the end of the course.

4   *BATPACK is limitation based.* The limitations of BATPACK are

deliberate and are made explicit. We are not attempting to provide training in behaviour therapy. Our sole aim is to train teachers in a limited number of key behavioural teaching skills and techniques for use in classroom teaching.

5 BATPACK is research based. The content of BATPACK units refers specifically to relevant research completed by our research team. This includes reference to our surveys of the prevalence of troublesome classroom behaviours, our behavioural observations of teachers' 'natural' rates of approval and disapproval and our demonstration studies of successful behavioural interventions. This means that all of the material presented is backed by research evidence rather than mere assertion or opinion. Moreover, the content and techniques employed are also the result of continuing experimental evaluation (see below).

6 *BATPACK is evaluation based.* From the outset, teachers who have attended BATPACK courses have been required, as part of the contract, to contribute to the evaluation of the package. As a result of constructive criticism from teachers and BATPACK tutors, many changes were made to the content and structure of BATPACK. Moreover, the effects of BATPACK training are expected to be demonstrable in terms of changes in teacher behaviour and pupil behaviour. Earlier versions were continually revised until BATPACK could meet these criteria. Experiments, involving independent classroom observers, have clearly demonstrated that BATPACK training achieves its objective of changing teachers' classroom behaviour and that this leads to improvements in children's behaviour. Typically, teachers on the course increase their use of approval and decrease their rates of disapproval and these changes, in turn, lead to the children in their classes spending far more of their time actually getting on with their work. More generally, our research emphasises that skills-based, in-service training is an effective means of passing on the benefits of the behavioural approach to practising classroom teachers.

BATPACK is designed to be taught by a tutor who has attended a special training course. Prospective tutors must have a good working knowledge of behavioural approaches to teaching and are usually educational psychologists, advisers or senior teachers. On the tutor training courses, tutors receive a copy of the BATPACK manual which contains all the instructions for running courses. Since the latest version was published in January, 1985 (Wheldall and Merrett,

1985) nearly 1,000 tutors have been trained in its use.

The BATPACK course consists of six one-hour sessions called units, taught at weekly intervals. For each unit there are five objectives. Every unit is divided into five elements so that each corresponds to an objective. The first objective is always a review item, giving the opportunity for students to ask questions and for the tutor to review aspects of the earlier units. The last objective of each unit is concerned with the practical assignments for the following week. These always include some reading and time for the student to observe and record his/her own behaviour in responding to the class. The three other elements are used to explore practical problems (identifying problem behaviours), to develop skills (pin-pointing, praising, observing) and to explain techniques (setting rules, defining work demands). Every unit has an accompanying 'take-home' in which an attempt is made to supply some of the theoretical material which will inform the practical skills learned in the unit and which provides the reading assignment for the week. In the last unit an attempt is made to review all the skills and techniques which have been covered and to present some successful classroom strategies tried out by other practising teachers.

A Small Scale Evaluation

BATPACK has been subjected to a programme of continual experimental evaluation, as mentioned earlier, and a number of these studies have been published. Wheldall, Merrett and Borg (1985) report a fully controlled experimental evaluation, and a case study evaluation is reported by Wheldall, Merrett, Worsley, Colmar, and Parry (1986). Merrett and Wheldall (1989) subsequently reported an evaluation study which included evidence that BATPACK training of teachers increases not only the amount of time their classes spend on-task but also increases the amount of academic work the children produce. Rather than detailing these studies at length we will describe briefly here, as an example, a more recent, small-scale experimental evaluation study of the latest version of the package. A detailed account of the development of BATPACK is provided by Wheldall and Merrett (1987b).

The study was carried out in a small primary school in Birmingham where the whole staff attended a BATPACK course. Five of the teachers attending agreed to be observed. Observations of teacher and class behaviours were collected before and following the course by trained research assistant, using our OPTIC schedule.

Before the course, the teachers' overall use of negative statements (reprimands) was greater than their use of positive statements (praise). Following the course over three times as many praise statements as reprimands were employed, on average. All teachers increased their use of praise, except one whose level was already far higher than that of the other teachers. All teachers dramatically decreased their use of reprimands, especially those contingent on social behaviour. Pupil on-task behaviour following BATPACK increased from 67% to 84%. Gains ranged from 4% to 28% and averaged 17%. In other words, children on average spent 25% more time working, following BATPACK training.

An attempt was also made to collect product data, i.e. evidence for change in quantity and quality of work produced by pupils. To this end, teachers were asked to set given essay topics to their classes with a 30-minute time limit. Only the teacher of the top junior class (of 10–11-year olds), however, was successful in collecting a sample of essays before and after the course. The mean on-task behaviour for this class for the writing session before the course was 71%, compared with 99% for the session following completion of the course. In the pre-course session, the children produced a mean of 116 words in the 30-minute session, while in the session following the course this had risen by over 30% to a mean of 152 words. As was found in the previous studies discussed earlier, increases in academic behaviour coincided with increases in on-task behaviour. These findings have been further replicated in a study by Merrett and Wheldall (1989).

The final version of BATPACK for use in primary schools is now widely available and it has been found to be effective in training primary-school teachers in key behavioural classroom management techniques. We are now extending our research and development and are working on new packages. The first is a version of BATPACK suitable for use in secondary schools and is entitled BATSAC (Behavioural Approach to Teaching Secondary Aged Children) (Merrett and Wheldall, 1988b). This package has undergone trials in both the UK and New Zealand and has just been made available for use by trained BATPACK tutors. The second is a follow-up package to BATPACK which will deal with more severe behaviour problems of particularly troublesome individual children. Work is in progress on this package and its working title is BRATPACK!

This chapter has been concerned with classroom behaviour management. Our aim has been to show that it is more productive and more effective to take a positive outlook and to focus on assisting pupils to increase their level of appropriate classroom behaviour, rather than dwelling on problem behaviours. But as we said earlier, a behavioural approach has more to offer teachers than just effective behaviour management. Our behavioural interactionist perspective views this as only one aspect of a more encompassing behavioural approach to teaching: helping children to learn academic skills and, in turn, to become effective, independent learners.

7

The Importance of Responsive Social Contexts

'A child is not a vase to be filled, but a fire to be lit.'

Rabelais

You may have heard the story of the 'self-made' man being interviewed by a TV journalist. 'Now Clive,' began the interviewer, "If we look back over your remarkable career, we see that not only did you write three best-selling novels, found a multi-million dollar company, and invent an engine that runs on fresh air but that you also play chess for your country, advise the government on economic matters and speak sixteen languages. To what do you attribute this impressive list of achievements?' 'Well,' said the man scratching his head, 'I didn't get much education, so I had to think a lot.'

In the early chapters of this book we emphasized our concerns about some aspects of contemporary schooling. We argued for the need for an altogether more positive orientation towards teaching. We also commented on the alien, artificial environments in which many children are expected to learn both appropriate social behaviour and important academic skills. So far, we have shown how classroom teaching can be made more positive, to the benefit of both teachers and children. We have outlined methods and procedures by means of which teachers can structure their classrooms, so that more time is likely to be spent academically engaged. This, in turn, means that academic learning of skills and knowledge is now more possible. We have brought about the necessary but not sufficient conditions for academic learning to take place. For even when time is spent 'academically engaged', not much real, worthwhile learning will occur unless the teaching and learning context is appropriately structured and the lesson content is matched to the needs of the children.

The quotation from Rabelais at the beginning of this chapter sums up our view of how learning should be structured for children; not so that we can stuff them full of 'knowledge' but to help them to learn to become independent learners. Unlike the man in our story, we would prefer to believe that powerful intellectual and academic skills might result from education rather than being seen as compensation for lack of education! Our recent classroom-based research has focused attention on social and interactive aspects of contexts in which children acquire intellectual and academic skills.

Educators are slowly and hesitatingly coming to appreciate that people learn to speak and read and write in contexts that are essentially social in character. Even before children learn to speak they are welcomed as communicators. Very young children can both communicate their needs to and elicit actions from other people. In this sense they already have a measure of control over their social environment, but learning to speak affords even greater control, through vastly increased opportunities for interaction with other speakers. Through the continued responsiveness of parents and other people in their immediate social environment, children learn the meaning of words and how to use language to gain the attention and assistance of others. Children, in effect, practise the use of language, not as a preparation or training for social life, but as social life itself, as Florio-Ruane (1983) has commented.

Several points can be made about the social context in which children learn to speak. First, control over initiating, continuing and ending language-interactions is shared between child and adult. Second, the task or the content of the language interaction is a genuinely shared one, that is, the task or content is meaningful and important to both parties, as in the case of a parent helping a child learn the names of family members. Third, there are reciprocal gains in skill for both children and parents. Children become increasingly skilled at using language, and adults become increasingly skilled at interpreting and responding to their children's emerging but as yet idiosyncratic language. This processs of interaction allows adults and children to learn to communicate more and more effectively. Fourth, the parent or adult, in responding to children's initiations, responds more as a supportive audience than as an external evaluator. These points stress the interactive social relationship between child and parent when a child is learning to speak.

On the basis of extensive reviews of many studies of early adult–infant interaction, Bronfenbrenner (1979) identified 'primary developmental contexts' as particularly powerful and effective contexts in which young children learn language and intellectual skills. Such contexts provide regular opportunities for a less skilled participant (e.g. a child) to engage in shared activities with a more skilled participant (e.g. a parent) with whom there is a positive social relationship. We have expanded Bronfenbrenner's concept to encompass the features of any responsive social context in which learning occurs (Glynn, 1985, 1987; Wheldall and Glynn, 1988).

A responsive social context is one in which control is shared between the less skilled and the more skilled participant and in which the more skilled participant adopts a responsive interactive role, rather than a controlling or custodial role. Interestingly, responsive social contexts for learning occur more frequently in natural settings, such as during household tasks (e.g. cleaning, washing, gardening) and on occasions such as shopping trips and outings. These contexts provide regular opportunities for brief, child-initiated, one-to-one interactions with an adult. The selection of the environmental setting is typically under the control of the adult. But the selection of particular topics, the specific time to initiate a request or question, and the ending of the brief interaction are under the control of the child. It is up to the adult to respond rather than initiate, since these contexts frequently arise when the adult is already engaged in some other task or activity. In contrast with home settings, school settings are often so designed that responsive social contexts seldom occur. Children may have little opportunity to initiate interactions, or to share a task with a teacher. If the relationship between teacher and child is not positive and mutually rewarding, there is little chance of establishing a responsive social context.

Unfortunately, teachers' well-intentioned efforts to provide remedial instruction seldom occur in responsive social contexts. Tightly structured and tightly controlled remedial programmes afford little opportunity for learners to initiate or to share control. Learning-tasks presented within such programmes are frequently imposed on the learner by a teacher as part of a tightly sequenced curriculum. Not only are such tasks not shared between teacher and learner, but they may even become meaningless and non-functional for both learner and teacher. Timing, presentation and sequencing of tasks is totally controlled by the teacher or the producer of the remedial programme. Many primitive behavioural approaches to remedial education could be criticized on these grounds.

Moreover, when children do initiate in such contexts, their comments may be viewed as distracting or counter-productive because they interrupt the pre-planned flow of lesson material. In these circumstances there is a danger that the teacher's role may become even more controlling. More and more teacher attention is given to keeping children complying with the requirements of the task. This may be met with increased resistance by children, which in turn may be responded to with still firmer controls being imposed by the teacher. In this way children with learning difficulties can be rapidly turned into children with behavioural difficulties. This makes it even more difficult for them to learn.

In our view, responsive social contexts can be characterized by three distinctive features:

1   they provide opportunities for children to initiate learning interactions
2   they allow for reciprocal gains in skills between children and teachers
3   they provide children with feedback that is responsive rather than corrective.

We will now examine each of these features in turn.

OPPORTUNITY TO INITIATE

If child-initiated learning is to be facilitated, then teachers must relinquish some of their direct control over children's behaviour. Teachers will need to learn how to wait for children to initiate, and then to respond positively to those initiations. They will also need to learn how to structure contexts which will promote children's initiations.

In the field of language learning a procedure known as Incidental Teaching has received extensive research support (Hart and Risley, 1980). Incidental Teaching requires that instead of prompting, questioning or giving instructions to children as a means of promoting language use, teachers allow the child to make the first move and respond appropriately to that initiation. We will examine research data in chapter 9 to see just how effective the Incidental Teaching procedure can be.

Similarly, in the context of learning to read, teachers should be less intrusive in their response to errors. The results of studies by Wheldall, Wenban-Smith, Morgan and Quance, 1988) (reported in chapter 4) clearly show that teachers rarely afford young or low-progress readers the chance to initiate self-correction of errors, since they invariably correct children's reading errors almost immediately. Research reviewed in the following chapter shows that by pausing for up to five seconds following an error, tutors allow children to initiate error correction procedures themselves and hence make more independent progress in learning to read.

An important and essential concomitant of encouraging children's initiatiops is a tolerance of and willingness to accept errors. Errors provide valuable opportunities for children to learn strategies of self-correction, as McNaughton (1988) has demonstrated. So-called errorless learning processes were the legacy of programmed learning to the behavioural objectives movement. Behavioural programmes involving errorless learning procedures are still evident today in Direct Instruction materials, commonly used with children who have learning difficulties. In our view these procedures restrict the opportunities for independent learning, particularly opportunities to learn to self-correct errors.

OPPORTUNITY FOR RECIPROCAL GAINS IN SKILL

This feature concerns the notion of a shared activity or shared task which is beneficial for both teacher and children. It also concerns the notion that both teacher and children increase in skill as a result of continued interaction around shared tasks. An example of a task which is beneficial for both parties is conversation, which a child learns through repeated brief language-interactions with a parent or teacher. The parent or teacher is learning to interpret tentative and imprecise child utterances in terms of the specific contexts in which they occur, and in terms of his or her detailed knowledge of that individual child. Growth in parent or caregiver skills in interpreting and responding to child language is paralleled by growth in the child's skill at using language. In this way, the conversational task is truly a shared one. Mutual improvement in skill is likely to enhance the positive social relationship between parent or teacher and child.

In many classroom and school learning contexts, children encounter very few opportunities to share an academic task with a teacher or tutor. Teachers are all too often totally occupied with giving instructions and monitoring whether children are complying with these instructions. There may be little opportunity for teachers to gain in skill as an outcome of extended interactions of this kind. In contrast, peer tutoring, for example, appears to offer important opportunities for mutual gains in skill between tutor and tutee, as we will see in chapter 8.

In peer tutoring situations, the degree of control over the learner by the tutor is well short of total control, because both are learning new skills from the interaction. However, there are many learning contexts where there is little benefit for the teacher. In these contexts, even one-to-one interaction with a teacher may be counter-productive. It is possible that the learner could be maintained in a state of 'instructional dependence', as McNaughton (1981) puts it. For example, learner compliance to more and more simple instructions may actually reinforce the teacher for providing more and more help. By providing more help the teacher is taking increasing control over the learning interaction. Unfortunately, this may occur particularly with children experiencing learning difficulties.

OPPORTUNITIES FOR RESPONSIVE FEEDBACK

In many learning contexts, teachers may be responding to accuracy at the expense of fluency by providing corrective rather than responsive feedback. When teachers use excessive corrective feedback for children's writing, for example, they may be extinguishing fluent writing. Excessive attention to accuracy of letter formation, spelling, syntax, may result in children producing minimal amounts of accurate but extremely limited writing.

In contrast, descriptive studies of children learning to speak suggest that corrective feedback is not widely used. Brown and Hanlon (1970) found that parents respond to the content of their children's speech, rather than to its form. Newly arrived immigrants would have a great deal of trouble acquiring a new language if local people responded to their language initiations with corrective feedback, rather than responding to the content and context of these initiations. Fortunately, hesitant attempts to seek information, to ask for directions or assistance are responded to by the community irrespective of the form of utterance, and immigrants learn to speak their new language by using it in context. However, some teachers may respond to children's language initiations with corrective rather than responsive feedback. This shifts the learning context from a responsive social one to a controlling supervisory one, in which further child initiations will be unlikely.

IMPLICATIONS FOR STRUCTURING LEARNING OPPORTUNITIES

From this focus on responsive social contexts, several implications may be drawn. First, teaching should take place in the context where the skills are to be used. If children are to learn to use language in the context of interaction with play materials or with other children or adults, then teaching should occur in those contexts. If children are to learn to read words and sentences from meaningful text materials, teaching should occur in the context of reading stories from books. However, such teaching should not be so intrusive as to impose the teacher's presence or prompting as the primary control over children's learning. In the case of oral language, children's initiations should be cued by a wide range of objects, events and activities that occur in everyday situations. In the case of reading, children's initiations (attempts at unknown words and at self-corrections) should be cued by words, sentences, themes and pictures in stories being read.

A second implication is that by teaching in everyday contexts, through using Incidental Teaching strategies, for example, teachers would be more likely to ensure generalization of children's learning. Teaching should take place in a richly varied stimulus environment, and should occur at varying times of the day, and in a variety of contexts, at least partly under the control of the child.

A third implication concerns the selection of types of learning tasks. It seems that shared tasks which allow for gains in skill for both the teachers and children may be especially fruitful. The practice of recruiting older children, who themselves may have deficits in performance, to provide responsive feedback for children who are performing at an even lower level would seem to be very worthwhile. This is discussed further in chapter 8.

The final implication concerns the importance of encouraging children to read, write and speak fluently, rather than insisting on complete accuracy too soon. This is particularly important since increases in elaboration and complexity of oral and written language appear to be closely related to fluent reading, speaking and writing. Maintaining fluency in language or other literary skills can be achieved through responsive feedback and does not require corrective feedback. Responsive feedback may be more readily implemented in natural settings and may itself promote further interaction between children and teachers.

In this brief chapter we have introduced the features of responsive social contexts which we believe are critically important for children's learning. We have noted the need for teachers to provide learning contexts which allow children the opportunity to initiate learning interactions, which allow for mutual gains in skill between children and teachers and which provide responsive rather than corrective feedback. In the following two chapters we examine the growing research evidence which supports each of these features within the context of improving children's reading, writing and oral language skills.

8

Responsive Contexts for Learning to Read

Can you remember learning to read? More than likely not; the fact that you are reading this book indicates that, in all probability, learning to read was, for you, a fairly straightforward process which has left few traces in your memory. It seems as if we could always read. But for some children, perhaps more than we would at first suppose, learning to read is not so simple. Here is an account of one child's experiences on the road to literacy.

'When I was a small boy, in the early fifties, I started my school career at an inner city church school in Derby and began to learn to read using the 'Happy Venture' series. I was soon involved, if not exactly engrossed, in the rather pedestrian doings of Dick and Dora and their pets, Nip and Fluff, all portrayed in the rather sombre black and amber illustrations which characterized post-war austerity.

About halfway through my infant-school career, my family moved to a new council housing estate on the outskirts of the town, and so when I was six I had to move to a new purpose-built infant school with a new reading scheme. The doings of 'Old Lob', a farmer, and his animals, replaced those of Dick and Dora and Nip and Fluff; not, as I recall, with any marked improvement in interest level. My teacher soon became worried about me. I could read 'Dick and Dora' but not much 'Old Lob'. In her terms, I was clearly 'behind' in my reading; a reading failure at six!

The exact details escape me now, but my mother soon learned of my apparent reading difficulties and took action. I come from a fairly traditional working-class background; my parents were not great readers and money was very short in those days. However, my mother bought a copy of 'Old Lob' from the educational stationers in town (an alien environment for us) and proceeded to hear me read every night. When we had finished the first book she bought the next.

Childhood memories can be unreliable but I remember vividly the one moment of glory in my school career. Sometime later, when reading to my teacher, we finished the first 'Old Lob' I had been set and she picked up the next level book. 'I've read that,' I said, probably sounding more confident that I felt, and proceeded to read it aloud correctly from cover to cover. My teacher clapped her hands for attention and announced, 'Class, this boy has read a whole book in one day.' From that day I became a 'star' reader in her eyes and, like so many self-fulfiling prophecies, soon a very competent one.

I subsequently developed a voracious appetite for books. Suffering from childhood asthma, I was often absent from school and spent many weeks propped up in bed, reading. Hearing of my appetite for books, people passed on boxes of (usually unsuitable) books for me to read. And that's how I came to read *Portrait of the Artist as a Young Man* by James Joyce when I was about 11; although it must be said I much preferred the saucy book I found in the same box entitled *A Widow for the Winter*! But that is another story . . . .'

Some things have not changed that much. We still undervalue the role of parents in teaching their children. It is currently fashionable to talk of parental involvement, but all too often this means parents organizing fund raising or mixing paint. But we have made some progress. Today it is commonplace for reading books to be sent home with children for parents to hear them read. But this is rarely carried out in any coherent or co-ordinated way, and few teachers would acknowledge that parents may be their child's most important tutor. The boy in the story above was fortunate in having a mother with the confidence to do what she did; otherwise he would not be writing books such as this one today. Many children are not so fortunate.

We have noted earlier, in chapter 3, the importance of ecological factors and setting events in influencing children's learning. We have described these under the heading of 'antecedent' conditions in our discussion of the ABC of teaching. In learning to read, ecological factors and setting events together contribute to the quality of the interactive learning context available for learners and teachers. In the present chapter, we examine specific ecological factors (e.g. the nature and difficulty of reading materials) and setting events (e.g. opportunity for children to read aloud individually to a teacher or tutor, who responds to their reading), and how they operate to influence the behaviour of children and teachers. We will also examine the role of selective reinforcement for independent reading. We will show how a behavioural interactionist perspective comes into its own as a powerful model for understanding aspects of the process of learning to read, and, more importantly, how we can structure responsive social contexts for more effective tutoring of reading. We will show how the role of the teacher is vital to this process but also how parents and classroom peers can be employed to great effect as reading tutors.

ECOLOGICAL FACTORS AND SETTING EVENTS IN LEARNING TO READ

Reading Material

The type of reading material we provide for young children will greatly influence the nature of the interaction between the teacher and the child. Providing a beginning reader with a set of flash cards is likely to be a setting event for provoking teacher questions such as 'what's this word?' Flash cards also provide a setting event for examining words in isolation and for children to make single word responses. Single word responses by children may in turn limit teacher feedback to a simple indication of correct or incorrect. In contrast, providing a beginning reader with a natural language text, even a very simple one, is likely to be a setting event for a much wider range of child and teacher behaviours. For example, the teacher may now require the child to point to words in sequence while reading the sentence. The teacher may ask the child to predict the meaning of an unknown word from the information available, not only from the graphic cues in the letters of the word, but also from the semantic and contextual cues provided by the other words in the sentence and in the whole story. In this context, teacher feedback might also provide children with information about the usefulness of their strategies for predicting or solving unknown words. Thus, different types of reading material function as setting events for quite different patterns of teacher–child interaction.

We believe that for young children learning to read, and for older low-progress readers, the most important setting event is regular opportunity to read meaningful passages from interesting books to an interacting listener. This view is supported by contemporary authorities on reading such as Smith (1978), Clay (1979) and McNaughton (1987). Ironically, this is the very setting event which may be denied to low-progress readers by remedial reading approaches which emphasize opportunities to practise letter and sound identification skills with isolated words. Allington (1983) has noted the paradox that classroom teachers may provide fewer opportunities for low-progress readers to read from text material than they provide for high-progress readers.

The level of difficulty of books is clearly another critical antecedent event influencing teacher and child interaction in reading. Books that are too difficult present so many new words that they become contexts for word-by-word reading and for excessive attention to graphophonic cues. They offer severely limited opportunities for children to employ semantic and contextual strategies to solve unknown words. Books that are too difficult may also impair the quality of teacher–child interaction. They may restrict opportunities for the teacher to observe and reinforce children's problem-solving behaviours, especially children's self-correction of errors. The high error rate resulting from books that are too difficult may set the occasion for a very aversive style of teacher–child interaction. This type of interaction is characterized by the teacher continually providing corrective feedback on errors and by the child learning to take as few risks as possible. This is definitely not a responsive social context.

Surprisingly, books that are too easy may also cause difficulties. They too can impair the quality of teacher–child interaction. The very low error rate will provide few opportunities for low-progress readers to employ problem-solving strategies for the teacher to observe and reinforce. Our behavioural interactionist approach to teaching emphasizes the need for continual monitoring of performance. In the case of reading, frequent checks on the accuracy of children's oral reading will provide data on whether the current book level is too difficult or too easy. The data reported in chapter 4 established that over half of the children participating in the descriptive studies of oral reading with their teacher were reading books that were too easy.

A related antecedent event in learning to read, which is easily provided by teachers, is a preparatory introduction and discussion of the material to be read. Research by colleagues in New Zealand has examined this issue. Wong and McNaughton (1980) demonstrated that a seven-year-old low-progress reader improved her accuracy and self-correction of errors on occasions when the teacher carried out in advance a simple discussion of the story to identify events, outcomes and unfamiliar words and concepts. These results have been confirmed in two further studies (Singh and Singh, 1984; Knott and Moore, 1988). It seems clear then that one-to-one reading sessions may well be made more effective learning contexts if the tutor takes the time to introduce the material to be read, perhaps by discussing the story and by pointing out words the child is unlikely to have encountered before. This simple antecedent procedure may provide a more effective means of improving reading accuracy than the more intrusive and time-consuming method of the teacher responding to errors as they occur.

Teacher Modelling of Silent Reading

A widely agreed goal of education is to foster in pupils an affinity for books and reading. Yet surveys show that children read comparatively few books and spend only a small amount of time reading (see, for example, Farquhar, 1987; Garvey and Hegarty, 1987; Whitehead, Capey, Maddren and Wellings, 1977). Consequently, once some of the basic skills of reading have been mastered, many teachers timetable quiet reading periods for their pupils, often on a daily basis, in an attempt to encourage reading for its own sake. During these periods children are expected to read silently a book that they have usually selected for themselves. Meanwhile, teachers may commonly busy themselves by engaging in classroom 'chores' (pinning up work, marking books, writing on the blackboard) or, more commonly, by hearing individual children read aloud. This can be distracting for the silent readers and may also become a context for other children to chat among themselves instead of reading. Bandura (1977) argues that most human behaviour is learned observationally through modelling, and that physical demonstration is the source of most social learning in children. This is especially true when behaviours are modelled by parents, teachers or other popular individuals. He found that when there was conflict between the model's behaviour and what was said, it was the behaviour and not the words that children were more likely to imitate. Ironically, teacher modelling of appropriate academic behaviour seldom occurs in classroom or school settings, but 'Do as I do' is, in our view, a much more effective teaching strategy than 'Do as I say.'

In recent years, teachers have been encouraged to create a time for quiet reading for both teachers themselves and for the class, when the children are not interrupted or distracted. At the same time the children are able to see the teacher demonstrating or modelling the desired behaviour of silent reading.

This practice of both teachers and children participating in regular silent, recreational reading sessions as part of the primary curriculum is becoming commonly referred to by the term Sustained Silent Reading (SSR) or Uninterrupted Sustained Silent Reading (USSR). USSR usually takes the following form:

1   Pupils should read quietly and a quiet reading atmosphere, free from distractions and interruptions, should be encouraged.
2   The teacher should also read, thereby providing an adult model for reading, but this should be recreational reading (i.e. reading for enjoyment) and not the reading of material such as reports, memos, etc.
3   Pupils should ensure that they have sufficient reading material to last the USSR session, as they should not disrupt the session to change their books.
4   The choice of reading material should be as open as possible and a wide range of books, magazines, etc. should be made available in the classroom.
5   No written reports or records should be required of pupils of any books read during USSR sessions, since pupils are likely to read more if they know that they will not have to write a report on every book they read.

McCracken and McCracken (1972) advocated sustained silent reading as part of their 'Reading is only the tiger's tail' (RIOTT) programme. They subsequently investigated thousands of reports from teachers about RIOTT programmes 'in an unscientific way' (McCracken and McCracken, 1978) and concluded that those teachers who reported having difficulty with the method were those who were not reading with the children. They concluded that all adults in the classroom need to read or it will not work. They also argue that children should be asked to do nothing that the teachers would not do willingly and naturally themselves, i.e. no book reviews, word lists, work sheets, etc.: 'what a teacher does during and after silent reading defines it for children.'

Behind the rhetoric, however, there were until recently very few carefully controlled experimental studies testifying to the effectiveness of USSR-type procedures. As part of the collaborative research we have been pursuing in New Zealand and the United Kingdom, we have begun to examine the effects of teacher concurrent modelling of reading on children's reading behaviour. Concurrent modelling involves a competent model (the teacher) providing a continual display of the target behaviour (reading) and hence a continuing opportunity for learners to imitate. We now report two studies carried out in New Zealand (Pluck, Ghafari, Glynn and McNaughton, 1984) and a series of four studies subsequently carried out in the UK (Wheldall and Entwistle, 1988), all of which provide evidence for the effectiveness of concurrent modelling of reading or USSR.

The first New Zealand study involved the five lowest and the five highest achieving readers in a class of eight- to nine-year olds during their daily 10 to 15-minute recreational reading sessions. All the children had access to self-selected reading books and were allowed to exchange books with other children or from the class library during the sessions. The children were initially observed during a baseline phase of seven sessions, where the teacher carried out administrative, non-reading tasks while children were expected to get on with their reading. Next an alternating treatments design was employed whereby the teacher modelled silent recreational reading during sessions 8, 9, 11, 13, and 15, while baseline conditions obtained during the four intervening sessions. Both low and high achievers showed increases in on-task behaviour from baseline to teacher modelling conditions. The low achievers made the greatest gains, from an average of 31% during baseline to an average of 65% during teacher modelling conditions, a mean increase of 34 percent. The highest achievers showed less striking gains, from an average of 69% during continuous baseline to an average of 85% during modelling conditions, a mean increase of 16%.

In the second study a highly competent nine-year-old reader was monitored at home where the parents and/or a grandparent modelled reading. The child had access to books he had chosen for himself and to books chosen for him by his family. His reading was monitored for 24 sessions during evenings when his parents and grandmother used the living room to talk and watch television. The child was free to bring his own books into the room to read. Afer a seven-day baseline period, additional books, selected by parents, were introduced into the room. This was followed by a period in which, in conjunction with the additional books, parents and grandmother all modelled silent reading of their own books. Finally, adult modelling of reading was withdrawn, but the provision of additional books continued.

Finally, adult modelling of books was again introduced. During baseline the child spent between 20 and 35 minutes reading books he had selected himself, and 5 to 15 minutes reading parent-selected books. He showed little increase in reading time either of self-selected or parent-selected material between baseline and the condition in which extra books alone were provided. However, his reading time increased to 60–70 minutes on self-selected material and 20–30 minutes on parent-selected material during concurrent adult modelling in the first phase. The time he spent reading dropped slightly when adult modelling was withdrawn and extra books alone were available again, but rose to 68–80 minutes on self-selected books and 27–34 minutes on parent-selected books when adult modelling was reinstated. When observed at follow-up after the study was finished, the child was reading his own selected books for twice as long as he had been at the original baseline, but he was reading parent-selected material for only minimally longer than at baseline. The effect was clearly more powerful in increasing reading time with self-selected books than with books selected by parents.

The main aim of the series of studies carried out in the UK was to replicate these findings in a different educational context, to determine whether teacher modelling of appropriate reading behaviour during USSR sessions in British classrooms would consistently lead to marked increases in the amount of time pupils spend actually reading. It was also important to find out if teacher modelling was the critical variable in USSR or whether the effect might be due simply to the increased quietness commonly found during USSR sessions.

Four studies were undertaken in two primary schools, with a third- and a fourth-year junior class in each school. In all four classes, 'silent' reading sessions were commonly held while the teacher usually listened to individual readers or did some other task in the classroom. During these studies, at the start of all sessions, the teachers announced clearly that a) it was to be a quiet reading time and b) the children were to read their own books. During baseline observations the teachers would either call for individuals to come out, or go and sit near a group and call individuals from the group to hear them read.

During the experimental phases when the teachers were modelling reading the children were informed that a) it was to be a quiet reading time; b) the teacher had his/her own book to read which was very interesting; and c) the teacher did not want to be disturbed. The teacher then sat reading his or her own book in a prominent position. Observation sessions using the OPTIC schedule lasted for the first 15 minutes of each daily reading session of 15 to 20 minutes' duration.

In the first study, lasting six weeks, an ABAB reversal design was employed with class A1, comprising 23 ten- to eleven-year olds. During the initial baseline phase, on-task behaviour averaged 50%. This figure rose to a mean of 73% during the phase when the teacher first modelled silent reading, an increase of 23%. Mean on-task behaviour dropped to 56% when baseline conditions were reinstated and rose again to 82% when the teacher again modelled silent reading, a mean increase of 26%.

This seemed good evidence for the effectiveness of USSR, but we had one or two reservations about the procedure adopted in this class and so we decided to run a second, bigger study with three classes. This study lasted eight weeks and involved class A2 (comprising 28 nine- to ten-year olds), class B1 (comprising 27 ten- to eleven-year olds) and class B2 (comprising 28 nine- to ten-year olds). This time a multiple baseline design was employed, so that the teacher modelling was introduced sequentially within the three different classes.

The results were clear. Class A2 had an initial baseline on-task behaviour mean of 53% which increased to 79% during the first USSR (teacher modelling) phase, a 26% increase. The mean dropped to 60% during a return to baseline phase and rose to 81% during the second USSR phase, a mean increase of 21%. Class B1 had an initial baseline on-task behaviour mean of 58%. This rose to 87% during the first USSR phase, an increase of 29%. The on-task mean dropped to 74% during the return to baseline phase. Finally, in class B2 mean on-task behaviour during the baseline was 58% and rose to 81% during the USSR phase, an increase of 23%. In short, the combined multiple baseline and reversal design provided strong evidence for the effectiveness of teacher modelling during USSR sessions. The USSR consistently brought about increases in on-task behaviour of between 20% and 30% in three different classrooms.

The third study was designed to provide detailed information regarding the number of individual pupils whose behaviour was influenced by teacher modelling of silent reading, since data from the previous two studies took the form of class averages. Further data were collected from ten children in class A1 who had taken part in the first study. A simple ABA reversal design was employed. Eight of the ten children observed in the individual study increased their on-task reading behaviour mean percentage when the teacher modelled silent reading. The percentage increase varied from 3% for the child with the highest mean baseline percentage (97%) to a 22% increase for the child with the lowest mean baseline percentage (57%). Child G had to be omitted from the analyses as a result of continual absences; and it was thought that child E's low on-task behaviour may well have been related to severe domestic problems which eventually resulted in her mother and two older sisters leaving home.

While the effects of teacher modelling during USSR sessions appeared to be clearly demonstrated in the first three studies it is possible that the effect may have been attributable in part to the quieter conditions obtaining when the teacher modelled reading, instead of hearing children read aloud. The process of hearing children read aloud may be distracting to the quiet readers or may provide 'cover' for non-work-related chatter to go unnoticed. Consequently, a fourth study was carried out with class A2. This study examined the hypothesis that quiet conditions alone would produce increased levels of on-task reading behaviour during USSR sessions i.e. without the teacher needing to model silent reading.

Following the end of the previous study in class A2, five baseline sessions occurred and then the teacher announced at the start of each session that he wanted the children to read quietly as he had some important writing to complete and did not want to be disturbed. He did not model recreational reading nor did he listen to children read, as he had done previously. He was clearly seen to be at his desk, writing out schedules of events, programmes and score tables for a forthcoming school sports day.

During the return to baseline phase, the mean on-task behaviour dropped back from its former 81% to 63%. When the second procedure (quiet conditions but without teacher modelling) was introduced, the mean on-task level rose to 74%, a mean increase of 11%. This level dropped back to 64% during the subsequent return to baseline conditions, but rose to 85% when the teacher again modelled reading, a mean increase of 21%. During the quiet conditions but without teacher modelling, the classroom was much quieter than during baseline conditions since the teacher did not call out for children to come to his desk and pupils did not disturb the quiet readers by going out to the teacher's desk and by reading aloud. The children were quiet and generally did not distract others. During this phase, levels of on-task behaviour were higher than for all baseline phases. Nevertheless, the on-task behaviour levels were not as high as for any of the phases when the teacher modelled silent reading. Clearly, quiet conditions alone are not as effective as quiet conditions accompanied by teacher modelling of reading. It appears that the increase in time spent in on-task reading during USSR sessions may be attributable to quiet reading conditions in part, but that teacher modelling also contributes strongly to the effect.

This series of studies, carried out with classes of British primary-aged children, replicated and extended the findings of the New Zealand studies. All of the teachers involved said that their pupils were reading more books than they usually did. This was partly as a result of them having more regular reading sessions, but was also because they spent more time actually reading during the USSR sessions. The series of studies also provides further evidence of the powerful effects of setting events on children's classroom behaviour and learning.

One to One Interactions

As we have noted in chapter 3, access to an interacting adult is a setting event exerting a powerful influence on children's learning. Brief episodes of individual attention within the classroom context are occasions for an important type of teacher–child interaction. Such interactions rarely occur during whole-class or small-group instruction. This one-to-one interaction allows the teacher to monitor and to provide immediate feedback to individual children on their current reading performance. However, the one-to-one setting can produce interactions that are either productive or counter-productive for children's learning.

Some teachers use one-to-one interaction solely as a context for evaluative assessment, concerned largely with detecting errors and making critical comments. These interactions may become settings for poor task performance and even avoidance and withdrawal. This could happen to children who are low-progress readers and who carefully avoid being called on to read to the teacher. Other teachers may use one-to-one interaction as a setting for providing children with individualized qualitative feedback on their reading. Teachers following a behavioural interactionist approach may also use the one-to-one setting as an opportunity for monitoring their own teaching strategies. We regard the one-to-one setting in oral reading as being a critical component of a reading programme for both reader and teacher. In this setting teachers can monitor and reinforce important independent reading behaviours in children; for example, the self-correction of errors.

The behaviour of the teacher during one-to-one oral reading may itself promote different child behaviours. Clay (1969) identified self-correction of errors as an important predictor of high progress in learning to read. She found that self-corrections occur more frequently with high-progress than with low-progress beginning readers. Our own research (McNaughton and Glynn, 1981) subsequently found that self-corrections occurred less frequently under conditions of immediate teacher attention to errors. Requiring the teacher to wait for a period of up to five seconds (or until children reached the end of the sentence) resulted in increased self-correction of errors and in increased reading accuracy. The delaying of teachers' attention appeared to provide a context in which children could detect and attempt to correct their own errors. In contrast, immediate teacher attention precluded all opportunity for children to correct their own errors. Yet attending immediately to errors is what teachers tend to do when they hear children read, as our research (reviewed in chapter 4) clearly showed (McNaughton, Glynn and Robinson, 1987; Wheldall, Wenban-Smith, Morgan and Quance, 1988). It is important to consider whether high-progress and low-progress readers become setting events for different types of teacher behaviour. Teachers may be more likely to attend to errors immediately, in the interests of 'helping' low-progress children but in so doing may deny them the opportunity to self-correct. Such teacher 'help' would then be reinforced by the children's imitation of the correct words supplied by the teacher. However, for high-progress readers teachers may be more likely to pause before attending to errors to see whether the children might self-correct. In this context teachers may then also reinforce children for self-correction. Again, our research on teachers monitoring young beginning readers and older low-progress readers supports this view (Wheldall, Wenban-Smith, Morgan and Quance et al., 1988); teachers paused after an error less often with low-progress readers than with high progress readers.

In the oral reading situations we have described above, the one-to-one context has clearly emerged as a setting event for mutually positive interaction, a truly responsive social context leading to gains in skill for both child and teacher. Perhaps this is why we sometimes see interested children lining up eagerly wanting to read aloud to their teacher. Teachers employing a behavioural interactionist approach should monitor whether all children in their class receive sufficient opportunities for such one-to-one interaction. In one class for children with behaviour and learning difficulties we found that the teacher spent the most time in one-to-one interaction with those children who made greatest reading progress. Children making the lowest progress received progressively less time in one-to-one interaction with the teacher! It takes close and careful monitoring for teachers to establish a) whether for each particular child their one-to-one interaction functions as a context for negative or for positive interaction, and b) whether some children are being denied access to this important learning context.

Teacher behaviour in the one-to-one oral reading context should also reinforce readers' self-regulatory skills and decrease their dependence on teacher correction of errors. To this end, our research since 1975 has led us to develop the set of reading tutoring procedures known as 'Pause, Prompt and Praise', which will be detailed in the following section. These procedures include a set of teacher cues and prompts as well as selective reinforcement for independent reading behaviours.

When children can read the word correctly before the teacher supplies it, they escape from total dependence on the teacher. Hence it is important for the teacher to detect and reinforce children's self-corrections (errors corrected with no teacher assistance), children's prompted corrections (errors corrected following a teacher prompt), and children's attempted corrections. Reinforcement procedures employed selectively in this way are focused on increasing children's problem solving strategies, and thereby on increasing their success at reading new words.

In contrast, as we noted earlier, teachers frequently immediately supply the correct word when a child makes an error. In this context teachers are likely to reinforce the child for dependent behaviour, such as stopping and looking at the teacher to solicit the correct word rather than working on the reading text to seek clues. Reinforcement of the child's imitation of the teacher's correct model is likely to reinforce the whole sequence of dependency. Our research in Birmingham, reported in chapter 4, confirms findings from an earlier study (McNaughton, Glynn and Robinson, 1981) that teachers neither pause nor reinforce independence sufficiently when they hear children read (Wheldall, Wenban-Smith, Morgan and Quance, 1988).

'PAUSE, PROMPT AND PRAISE'

The 'Pause, Prompt and Praise' procedures embody all of the principles outlined above (Glynn, McNaughton, Robinson and Quinn, 1979; McNaughton, Glynn and Robinson, 1981, 1987). These procedures have been shown to be particularly effective when used by parents, peers and others tutoring low-progress readers, as we shall see (Glynn and McNaughton, 1985). The procedures were developed from our own continuing research on reading (described above) but also owe a great debt to the earlier reading research of Professor Marie Clay (reported, for example, in her book *Reading: the patterning of complex behaviour*, 1979, and in the 'Reading Recovery Programme', a nationwide programme in New Zealand for providing additional assistance to childen making low progress in reading after one year at school). Basically, Clay argues that in learning to read, children learn various strategies for predicting and working out unknown vocabulary. Learning to read is seen as a process which includes making mistakes (often referred to as reading errors or miscues) and gradually developing efficient strategies using both contextual cues, which relate to meaning and syntax, and graphical cues, which relate to the visual pattern of letters and words. As individuals learn to read they gradually manage increasingly more difficult reading material and so become independent readers.

In the Pause, Prompt and Praise procedures there are two important requirements of reading teachers or tutors. The first is to provide reading material at an appropriate difficulty level such that the children experience a context in which they encounter some unfamiliar words but know enough words to be able to make good predictions, even if these are miscues. The appropriate difficulty level of reading material can be broadly assessed by checking the child's rate of reading accuracy. If this rate is below 80% the text is too difficult; if the child is reading at over 95% accuracy it is clearly too easy. At a rate of between 90% and 95% accuracy, promotion to the next level should be seriously considered. Thus, an ideal context for children learning to read, with all the advantages of making mistakes, is between 80% and 90% accuracy.

The second important requirement of reading tutors is that they should provide appropriate feedback as they listen to the child read. It is important to stress that mistakes (errors, miscues) are to be expected. All children learning to read make mistakes; it is an important part of the process. In other words, making mistakes is a good thing. By carefully monitoring the child's response to text the teacher can readily work out if the child is making average, or even rapid, progress and if he or she is using efficient predictive strategies. Self-correction is seen as an indicator that children are reading actively in that they are able to detect that they have made an error, and to 'solve' problem words independently.

The Pause, Prompt and Praise tutoring procedures require the tutor to do just that: pause – prompt – praise. We provide below a very brief summary of the procedures, but full details are provided in a simple booklet for parents, *Remedial Reading at Home: helping you to help your child* (Glynn, McNaughton, Robinson and Quinn, 1979).

Pausing. When the child makes an error or hesitates it is important for the teacher or tutor to pause for at least five seconds. This allows the child a reasonable opportunity to correct his or her own error. Pausing is difficult for most reading tutors, but it is a key factor in responding helpfully to the child who is learning to read. It is particularly hard where the child is a low-progress reader, and where the teacher or tutor wants to provide as much help as possible.

Prompting. If, after a pause of five seconds, the child has made either no response or has made an error, the tutor then prompts.

The type of feedback or prompt given depends on the nature of the error. If the child's error has not made sense then the prompt should be aimed at providing clues about the meaning or context of the story; for example, a question like "Well, do you think the word would be "horse" when the story is about the place where we live?' Often the child's miscue makes sense but the word is still not correct; for example, the child reads 'may' where the word is 'might'. In examples like these the tutor's prompt should be aimed at helping the child to look again at the graphical features of the word; that is, how it looks. However, should the child hesitate and still make no attempt, the tutor can either ask the child to read on to the end, or from the beginning of the sentence. Often this additional context provided by the other words in the sentence will help the child to work out the unknown word. In many cases this type of prompt is sufficient for children to determine the correct word. In the few instances where children are not able to correct these errors after one or two prompts, it is suggested that they are then told the word. This prevents the interruptions to the child's reading from becoming too long.

Praising. Finally, teachers or tutors should reinforce appropriate reading behaviour. As we have argued, however, reinforcement should be used both contingently and selectively. It is important to note that the praising of correct reading should be in the form of a specific, descriptive comment rather than just a comment like 'Good boy.' For example, 'Good work David. You corrected "rabbit" all by yourself' tells David exactly what he is being praised for, and so the praise is contingent upon independent reading behaviour. It is important to reinforce children for appropriate independent reading behaviours such as self-correcting or working out a word following a prompt as well as for, say, reading a whole sentence or paragraph correctly.

Our first research study evaluating the effectiveness of the Pause, Prompt and Praise technique was carried out in an Auckland suburb in 1978. It was called the Mangere Home and School Project and it involved the intensive study of 14 families (McNaughton, Glynn and Robinson, 1981). Low-progress readers aged 8 to 12 years with reading deficits from two to five years were tutored at home three times a week for 10 to 15 minutes by their parents. Books of appropriate difficulty, and with stories of interest to the older children, were selected and provided by the project. Continual monitoring from tapes of children's reading enabled the researchers to supply books of increasing difficulty levels as children's accuracy improved. After 10 to 15 weeks, results showed that children, on average, made nearly six months' reading progress, despite the fact that they had been making little or no progress before the project. On average their rate of self-correction nearly doubled.

The original study clearly showed that parents were able to change their own natural tutoring style following training and feedback from the researchers. Typically, as untrained tutors, parents rarely commented on correct reading or the child's attempts to solve unfamiliar words. They tended not to pause but rather to provide the child with the correct word immediately following the child's hesitation or error. In summary, as untrained tutors working with their own children with reading difficulties, they did not pause or prompt or praise. Interestingly, the data collected showed that their untrained tutoring had little effect on their children's reading. However, following training in these methods and regular feedback sessions from the researchers, parents learned to delay their attention to children's errors (i.e. pause) and to provide appropriate prompts or cues instead of simply telling the word. They also greatly increased their use of praise.

The Mangere Home and School Project was so successful with children who were older low-progress readers that the techniques were subsequently presented on New Zealand Television and the parent booklet was widely distributed. The original study has now been replicated successfully many times (Glynn and McNaughton, 1985), in New Zealand, Australia and in the United Kingdom. Twelve studies completed up to 1985 involved a total of over 100 tutors and 98 children between the ages of seven and twelve. All the subject children had marked deficits in reading skills varying from six months to as much as five years, with a mean of about two years.

Detailed results of these studies are now included in the recently revised monograph (McNaughton, Glynn and Robinson, 1987). We present here only a general summary of the data obtained from the 12 studies, which analysed tapes of parents and children reading together before and after training was given in the correct use of Pause, Prompt and Praise. Prior to training, parent tutors paused in response to a child's error for less than 33% of available opportunities. They responded by providing some kind of prompt (rather than supplying the correct word) for less than 47% of available opportunities. Their use of praise was extremely sparing. About eight praise comments, on average, occurred per 15-minute session. Following training in implementing the procedures, parents made gains in their use of pausing, prompting and praising of the order of two or three times their pre-training rates. However, the overall proportion of children's errors responded to did not change markedly, indicating that parents were easily able to improve the *quality* of their one-to-one interaction with children and did not simply respond to more errors.

Reported gains in children's reading ranged from 1.5 to 2.0 months in reading age per month of tutoring with Pause, Prompt and Praise (in one study) to 10.0 to 11.0 months in reading age per month of tutoring. These gains were evident both on standardized test measures and in session-by-session reading of test material. Similar gains were reported from studies measuring changes over time made in reading by individual children, and from studies comparing the performance of children in experimental and control groups. Analyses of data further showed that the amount of gain made by children reading was much greater when parents were using Pause, Prompt and Praise than when they were trying to help their children read on a one-to-one basis but without training in Pause, Prompt and Praise. For children who were of upper primary age and older, and who were up to five years behind in their reading, the responsive social context provided by the Pause, Prompt and Praise procedures resulted in major reading gains.

PEER-TUTORING USING 'PAUSE, PROMPT AND PRAISE'

Children with limited reading skills are clearly disadvantaged and this disadvantage will compound throughout their school careers unless some teaching strategy is tried which allows them to improve, and to improve quickly. The secondary curriculum, in particular, will be largely unavailable to slow or poor readers unless they make dramatic progress in reading. They need programmes which will enable them to achieve accelerated improvement in order to catch up with their peer group in reading skills: programmes of individual tutoring. It is the peer group itself which may hold one essential solution to the problem.

Without wishing to minimize the importance of the role of parents in the education of their children, we would like to argue the case also for the increased utilization of peers for tutoring of reading in addition to parents. We are using the term 'peer tutoring' here to mean tutoring by other young people of the same age or older than the tutees. Given adequate training, peers, just as effectively as parents or teachers, can learn to provide a responsive social context for tutoring reading.

Our reasons for advocating the increased use of peers are as follows:

1 Parents may not always be available in sufficient numbers nor may they be willing to volunteer for training, believing that they do not have the necessary skills.
2 Peer tutors are a plentiful resource available in every school. They will frequently volunteer for training and their tutoring can be readily monitored and organized.
3 It has been shown that low-progress readers respond readily to peer tutors – as well as, if not better than, they do to parents.
4 Tutoring has also been found to be beneficial to the peer tutors as well as to their tutees. Helping somebody to improve reading skill leads to improvement in the reading performance of the tutor at the same time.

Where tutors themselves are experiencing difficulties in reading, albeit at a higher level than the difficulties experienced by the tutees, there is a greater degree of mutual gain resulting from sharing the reading tasks than is the case with most parent tutors. There can be a greater sharing of control over the interactions when tutor and tutee each have room for improvement in reading skill. By having to implement Pause, Prompt and Praise procedures, the tutor becomes just as actively engaged in the reading material as is the tutee. Our observations of the developing positive relationships between tutor and tutee as they learn to read together suggests that peer tutoring of reading can provide excellent examples of responsive and interactive contexts for learning. We have carried out a number of studies of peer tutoring in both New Zealand and the UK.

In an early New Zealand study (Limbrick, McNaughton and Glynn, 1985), three underachieving 7- to 8-year-old readers (tutees) were paired with three volunteer 10 to 11-year-old tutors who were also underachieving. This study did not involve the Pause, Prompt and Praise procedure. Instead, it employed the procedures known as 'paired reading' (Morgan and Lyon, 1979) where tutor and tutee read aloud concurrently and the tutee taps on the table when he or she feels able to finish a sentence without further tutor support. Tutors cease reading aloud when a tutee taps, and resume reading aloud when an error occurs. Reading gains of between one and two years in reading age and level of book read were found for both tutors and tutees over a three month period. These gains occurred in both reading accuracy and comprehension, and were demonstrated both on standardized tests and on continuous daily measures of oral reading. Furthermore, both tutee and tutor children made reading gains far in excess of those made by samples of children from their two respective classrooms. Topping (1987) has reviewed outcome data from ten studies of peer tutoring using 'paired reading' procedures. Readers are also referred to Topping (1988) for an overview of peer tutoring.

Our programme of research on peer tutoring in the UK began in 1981. These studies were the first to employ the more conceptually systematic and supportive Pause, Prompt and Praise procedures with peer tutors. The first (unpublished) study was a small-scale, pilot investigation of peer tutoring. Three groups of three seven- to eight-year-old children took part in the study. They were all less delayed in their reading skills than the children in the original Mangere study, being only about six to 18 months behind in terms of reading age. One group was not tutored, a second group was tutored by untrained peers, while the third group was tutored by peers trained in the

Pause, Prompt and Praise method. The peer tutors were six 10- to 11-year-old pupils of at least average reading ability from the same school. Children in both tutored groups received about 30 individual tutoring sessions of about 10 to 15-minutes each over a period of ten weeks.

One child from the 'trained tutor' group dropped out half-way through the study, and this made overall comparisons difficult to interpret. What was clear, however, was that peers could be effectively trained to use all components of the Pause, Prompt and Praise procedure. Another interesting point which arose from this study is whether young children of this age who are not very far behind with their reading really need trained tutoring of the kind provided by the Pause, Prompt and Praise procedures. We will return to this point again shortly. The results of this study were equivocal, but it served as a valuable introduction to the rigours of this methodology and the practicalities of its implementation.

Our second UK study involving peer-tutors (Wheldall and Mettem, 1985) was, however, highly successful. We were able to demonstrate large gains made by 12-year-old low-progress readers when tutored by 16-year olds trained in the Pause, Prompt and Praise procedures. In brief, eight 16-year-old, low-achieving pupils were trained to tutor reading using these procedures. The effectiveness of training such tutors was investigated through a tutorial programme in which these older pupils then tutored eight 12-year-old remedial children who were on average three to four years behind in terms of reading age. The programme consisted of 24 tutorial sessions, each of 15 to 20 minutes, three days per week over eight weeks. Two matched control groups of remedial readers were also included in the study. One consisted of eight pupils tutored by a group of eight untrained tutors who taught during the same sessions and used the same materials. The second control group consisted of a third group of remedial readers who read silently, without a tutor, for the same amount of time as the other groups.

Analyses of the tutoring sessions revealed important differences in tutoring behaviour between the trained and untrained peer tutors. Attention to errors in both groups was very similar, at around 75%; but for delayed attention to errors (pausing), the picture was markedly different. Whereas the trained tutors paused following 58% of reader errors, tutors in the control group virtually did not pause at all. Prompting very seldom occurred in the untrained control group and was never successful when it did. In contrast, trained tutors used prompts in 27% of their attention to errors and were successful in

49% of these prompts. Finally, use of praise was observed on average 8.8 times per tutor per session in the trained tutor group, but hardly ever in the control tutor group. From these results it can reasonably be claimed that the experimental tutor group were trained successfully in the Pause, Prompt and Praise procedures.

Turning next to the performance of the tutees, it was found that children in the experimental group (who received trained tutoring) self-corrected around 20% of their errors, but for the control group this figure never rose above 10%. Moreover, the experimental group progressed through a total of 36 book-levels during the programme compared with 29 levels for the tutored control group and 24 levels for the untutored control group. Finally, the experimental group of tutees, who had a mean pre-test reading age of 8 years 4 months, made a mean gain of 6 months in reading accuracy by the end of the programme. The tutees of control group 1, who had received tutoring from untrained tutors, made a mean gain of 2.4 months. The pupils of control group 2, who read silently without a tutor, made a mean gain of 0.9 months. Similar gains were shown for reading comprehension. Half of the tutees in the experimental group made gains in excess of 6 months, while none of the tutees in either of the control groups made such gains. This study clearly showed that older low-progress readers could be successfully tutored by peers, providing the tutors had been given adequate training in these rigorous tutoring procedures.

The Wheldall and Mettem study has been described in some detail because the following four studies, which confirm and extend these findings, share similar aims and methodology. In essence, in attempting to demonstrate the effectiveness of peer tutoring of reading using Pause, Prompt and Praise procedures, the performance of both tutors and tutees is compared before, during and following the period of tutoring. More specifically, the tutoring behaviours of the tutors and the reading behaviours of the tutees form the basis of comparisons between experimental and control groups. In all four studies, the experimental groups included tutors who were specifically trained to use the Pause, Prompt and Praise tutoring procedures with their tutees. The main control groups involved tutors who were not trained to use Pause, Prompt and Praise, and who received only general advice as to how to tutor their tutees. In the first of the studies a second control or comparison group was included, which comprised readers at a similar level of reading performance as the tutees in the experimental and control groups who did not receive peer-tutoring during the course of the study. This series of replication studies will be reported in detail in Wheldall, Kift, Fox, Jeavons and Hack (in preparation).

The first replication study was carried out in a small junior school in the West Midlands, serving a large council housing estate. Ten 11-year-old fourth-year pupils of average or above average reading ability were selected as peer tutors. The study also involved 15 low-progress readers from third- and fourth-year classes aged nine to eleven years who were, on average, just over two years behind in their reading. The 15 low-progress readers were randomly allocated to three groups. Both tutored groups (trained and untrained) experienced six weeks of tutoring of three 30-minute sessions per week, i.e. 18 sessions in all.

All tutees were tested on the Neale Analysis reading test just prior to and then following the six-week period of tutoring. It should be noted, however, that a further two weeks elapsed before post-testing, making a total of two months between testings. The experimental Pause, Prompt and Praise group made a mean gain of 6.2 months for reading accuracy, whereas the control group receiving untrained tutoring gained 3.0 months, and the untutored comparison group 2.0 months. Similarly, for reading comprehension, the experimental group gained 8.4 months, the control group 4.4 months and the comparison group 3.4 months. All experimental subjects gained at least 6 months for both accuracy and comprehension over the two month period between testings, with the exception of one child who gained only five months for accuracy but 13 months for comprehension. In each of the other two groups only one child made a gain of 6 months or more, and this was only for comprehension (for accuracy no one gained more than 4 months). Another indicator of reading progress is promotion to higher book-levels. The results for this indicator parallel those for reading age. The experimental group on average progressed 6.2 levels, the control group 4.2 levels and the comparison group 2.6 levels. The two groups of tutors, however, made very similar gains in reading age. Mean gains for both groups of tutors for accuracy and comprehension were between 6 and 7 months. It can thus be seen that peer tutoring clearly benefits tutors as well as tutees.

We turn now to the results based on analyses of the taped tutor–tutee reading interactions. Recordings were made prior to (baseline) and following training in the Pause, Prompt and Praise procedures. Attention to errors was high in both groups, at over 80% during both baseline and experimental phases. During the baseline phase there was little evidence for 'pause', 'prompt' or 'praise' tutor behaviours in either group, as we have come to expect; and partly as a result of this low levels of self-correction on the part of tutees were observed. This picture did not change markedly for control group tutors during the intervention phase.

Following training in the Pause, Prompt and Praise procedures, however, the tutoring behaviours of the experimental group of tutors changed markedly. Delayed attention (pausing) was given in response to 56% of tutee errors, being partly responsible for the increase in tutee self-corrections to 20%. 67% of tutee errors were responded to with appropriate forms of prompt, and 64% of such prompts were successful in eliciting a correct response from the tutee. Finally, praise, which was virtually non-existent during baseline, now averaged five statements per session. This study thus established that fourth-year junior school pupils can be taught to tutor third- and fourth-year low-progress peers to good effect, yielding appreciable gains for both tutees and tutors. This provides additional support for the view that peer-tutoring programmes are also beneficial for tutors.

Our second replication study in the series, carried out again in a comprehensive school in the West Midlands with older children, comprised a simple comparison of the effects of trained and untrained tutoring. Ten fourth-year secondary-school pupils aged 14 to 15 years tutored 10 second-year low-progress readers aged 12 to 13 years who were between three and five years behind in their reading. Tutors and tutees were randomly allocated to two groups. One group of tutors was trained to use the Pause, Prompt and Praise procedures, while the other group received only general advice. Both groups of low-progress readers were tutored for 15 minutes, three times per week for five weeks. All tutees were tested on the Gapadol reading comprehension test (designed for use with older children) prior to and following the five-week tutoring programme. In brief, the group receiving trained tutoring made a mean gain of 11.5 months of reading age whereas the control group gained 7.5 months on average. All five low-progress readers in the trained tutoring group made gains of at least 10 months compared with only two children in the untrained group.

The reading performance of the tutors was not measured in this study, but again there were clear differences in tutoring behaviour. No instances of pausing, prompting or praising were recorded in either group prior to training and, as expected, there was little change in the behaviour of the untrained group over the tutoring programme. For the trained tutors, however, average levels of tutoring behaviours increased during the programme. Pausing averaged 62% and prompting 72% (successful on 73% of occasions). Praise averaged 6.4 instances per session and tutees self-corrected on 30% of available occasions.

The third replication study was also carried out in a comprehensive school in the West Midlands and again involved a comparison of two randomly allocated groups of six tutors and tutees. The tutors were twelve 15-year-old fourth-year pupils who tutored twelve first-year pupils aged 11 to 12 years with an average reading age of about eight years. They were thus three to four years behind in reading. The trained and untrained tutors tutored their low-progress readers for 26 sessions over eight weeks. Attention to errors was high, averaging over 90% in both groups of tutors over the programme, but tutoring behaviours in the untrained group remained at very low levels. Training was successful in changing the behaviour of the trained group, however, with pausing averaging 85% over the programme, prompting averaging 55% (92% successful) and praise averaging 3.5 instances per session. Tutee self-corrections for this group averaged 40% as against 11% in the other group, suggesting that the changes in tutor behaviour were bringing about changes in reader behaviour as a result. Testing prior to and following the tutoring programme on Neale Analysis showed that the low-progress readers in the trained tutoring group made average gains of 7 months in reading accuracy and 21 months in reading comprehension, compared with only 2 months and 10 months respectively for the untrained group. Again in this study tutors were not tested, but the results confirm the effectiveness of the Pause, Prompt and Praise procedures in bringing about rapid progress in reading skills in low-progress readers.

The fourth replication study is particularly interesting since it was not so successful! This study, carried out in a large middle school in the West Midlands, involved twenty 13-year-old tutors and twenty 9- to 10-year-old tutees who were, on average, only one year nine months behind in reading. Again the children were allocated randomly to trained and untrained groups and a tutoring programme of 27 sessions was implemented over nine weeks. For both groups, attention to errors was high, averaging over 70% over the programme but tutoring behaviours in the untrained group, as in the other studies, remained at low levels. In the trained group, pausing averaged 71% over the programme, prompting averaged 76% (64% successful) and praise averaged four instances per session. Tutee self-corrections for this group averaged 38% as against 19% in the untrained group. Testing prior to and following the tutoring programme on Neale

Analysis showed that the low-progress readers in both groups made average gains of 7 months in reading accuracy. For reading comprehension, the trained group gained 12 months on average whereas the untrained group gained 9 months.

The results of this last study were similar to those obtained from another of our unpublished studies, carried out in the UK with parent tutors. One of our students evaluated a parent tutoring programme with high-progress young readers. Three groups, each of seven pupils, were involved this time. The children were aged from $5\frac{1}{2}$ to $7\frac{1}{2}$ with reading ages in advance of chronological age by as much as $2\frac{1}{2}$ years. One group were an untutored comparison group, one group were tutored by their parents, who were given general tutoring advice, while the third were tutored by their parents who had been trained to use Pause, Prompt and Praise. Pre-training (baseline) and post-training measures of parental tutoring behaviours were obtained from both (tutored) groups.

Briefly, the results again showed that tutors (this time parents) could be readily trained to use the Pause, Prompt and Praise procedures. Before training, rates for pausing, prompting and praising were very low in both groups of parents but following instruction in the methods, the trained group paused after nearly 90% of hesitations or errors, prompted nearly 50% of the time (with 60% success) and used six times as much praise. The group of parents given only general advice made only marginal gains in these skills. Interestingly enough, however, the results showed that for these young skilled readers, trained parental tutoring using Pause, Prompt and Praise led to no greater gains in reading age than the general tutoring advice given to the other group of parents. Our interpretation of the results from these last two studies is that in contrast to the low-progress readers in the earlier studies, these readers may have already learned a range of strategies for predicting unknown words, and for self-correction of errors. For these readers, additional tutor input may be quite unnecessary.

Consistent with our concern that children learn independent reading skills, we believe remedial teaching procedures should provide no more support and assistance than is really needed. Another of our New Zealand studies with the Pause, Prompt and Praise procedure (O'Connor, Glynn and Tuck, 1987) illustrates this. The study involved 18 low-progress primary school readers in a residential setting. Staff were trained to implement first a minimal support Practice Reading procedure, and second the Pause Prompt and Praise procedures, but only if readers had shown insufficient progress with the Practice

Reading procedure alone. Careful monitoring of reader and tutor data was undertaken to ensure that where regular opportunity to read appropriate level texts to an interested and encouraging tutor proved sufficient for children to make progress, no further procedures were introduced. Over a six-week period, readers who received remedial assistance (whether Practice Reading or Practice Reading plus Pause, Prompt and Praise) made gains of 6 to 7 months on a standard test of reading accuracy, gains of 4 to 5 months on a standardized test of reading comprehension, and of 9 to 11 months on an informal prose measure. These gains were far in excess of the minimal gains made by a comparison group of children over the same period.

The Pause, Prompt and Praise procedures have been implemented much more widely than in the research studies we have reviewed in this chapter. In New Zealand and in the UK, educational psychologists and resource teachers have been using the procedures as part of their case work and consultancy work in schools and with parents. For example, one New Zealand educational psychologist, John Medcalf, was referred three 10- to 11-year-old low- progress readers in an urban intermediate school.

Instead of simply adding three more names to his ever-increasing case load, he offered to train two teachers in the school in how to use Pause, Prompt and Praise, and in how to establish a peer tutoring programme (Medcalf and Glynn, 1987). The teachers first learned the procedures themselves with the assistance of the psychologist, and then trained three volunteer children aged 11 to 12 years, who were also low-progress readers, to implement the procedures. Three pairs of children were formed and met for 15 minutes approximately three times per week, during which tutors implemented Pause, Prompt and Praise with their tutees. These sessions were tape-recorded so that the teachers could learn, monitor and provide feedback for the tutors on their implementation of Pause, Prompt and Praise and monitor the accuracy and self-corrections of the tutees. Standardized tests of reading accuracy and comprehension, and a local prose inventory of reading passages of increasing difficulty, were administered before and after a ten week period. Both tutors and tutees made gains in reading accuracy, reading comprehension and book levels read, ranging from one to three years. Interestingly, the first pair both made gains of one year, the second pair made gains of two years, and the third pair made gains of three years. This suggests that there may be links between the amount of gain made by tutors and the amount made by tutees. Learning to improve one's reading with Pause, Prompt and Praise is definitely an interactive process.

Currently our research programme in New Zealand is addressing the issue of how to train tutors to implement Pause, Prompt and Praise. Third-year trainee primary teachers were required as part of their teacher training programme to learn to teach the procedures to parents who would tutor their own children. This strategy represented a small step towards preparing teachers for working in partnership with parents. First, the trainees themselves learned to implement the procedures by working directly with a low-progress reader. Next they were each introduced to parents who had volunteered to tutor their own children using Pause, Prompt and Praise. In a first study (Henderson and Glynn, 1986) we designed and evaluated a feedback procedure for assisting trainee teachers to improve their training of parent tutors. Under baseline conditions the trainees were simply asked to do whatever they could to help parents learn the procedures, by referring to specific examples of tutoring which occurred in their most recent tutoring session. Baseline data showed that trainees virtually *told* the parent tutors directly what they had done, and what they ought to have done, with each instance of tutoring that occurred. They allowed parent tutors very little opportunity to remember procedures they had used with a specific reader error or to explain why they had selected the procedures they used. In short, trainees used an extremely intrusive form of prompting, which left parents little room to take any initiative or responsibility for their own learning. Following the introduction of a simple feedback procedure, which incorporated a range of much less intrusive prompts, trainee teachers were able to give parents much greater opportunity to remember and explain their own tutoring behaviours, and to self-correct these behaviours where appropriate. We believe this assisted parents to learn the tutoring procedure and to become less dependent upon trainee support in working with their own children. Further studies are underway to confirm the effectiveness of the feedback procedure in assisting other Pause, Prompt and Praise tutors.

CONCLUDING COMMENTS ON 'PAUSE, PROMPT AND PRAISE'

From the studies completed to date we can begin to draw tentative conclusions. It appears that both parents and peers can learn to use Pause, Prompt and Praise procedures relatively quickly and easily. Peer tutors have also been shown to gain in reading skill as a result of their tutoring. However, it seems that children who are making good or average (or even a little below average) progress do not really need trained tutoring. Simply having someone hear them read regularly appears to be enough. We should not provide more support than is necessary if we are to encourage independence. For older low-progress readers about to enter or already attending secondary school, however, it is a different matter. For pupils such as these, trained tutoring using Pause, Prompt and Praise has been shown (specifically) to be extremely effective, leading to major gains.

We reiterate that the issue of book-level is critical. A child who can read only three or four words from a ten word sentence has little chance of being able to utilize contextual cues, whereas a child who knows eight or nine of the ten words has a much higher chance of predicting the unknown words, especially when given a contextual prompt. A child, however, who can read nearly every word in the book has little chance to make progress in this important skill of predicting unrecognized words from contextual and graphophonic cues. The implication of this is that book-level is at least as important as the tutoring methodology; in fact, the effectiveness of the tutoring methods is contingent upon appropriate book-level. Prompting (especially contextual prompting) will be less effective where error rates are high, and cannot occur at all if no errors are made.

We would like to emphasize the all-important role of skilled, trained teachers in successfully implementing Pause, Prompt and Praise tutoring with parents and peers. We are keen to see tutoring skills 'given away' to non-professional tutors but are reluctant to allow benefits to be 'thrown away' by insufficient attention to detail, especially with regard to initial placement and promotion in book-level. In our view, the teacher should be responsible for this, albeit with the full collaboration of parents or peer tutors, for it is too critical to be left open to error.

Far from demeaning the reading teacher or 'taking bread from the teachers' mouths', there is, in fact, an important, professional and skilled role for the teacher to play in establishing and monitoring tutoring programmes. As well as taking the initiative in publicizing the approach and in setting schemes in motion, the teacher will be responsible for training tutors, for record keeping, for initial placement and subsequent promotion of children to appropriate book-levels, for giving feedback on tutoring performance and so on. Parents and peers are extremely valuable resources for the effective tutoring of reading with low-progress readers, but the success or failure of any such tutoring programme will hinge upon the professional skills of teachers.

Finally, the Pause, Prompt and Praise context described in this chapter illustrates the role of a responsive social context which allows learners a measure of control over their own learning. The context is responsive or interactive in that it allows low-progress readers to receive reading material of optimum difficulty and continues to supply texts of increasing difficulty in response to reader progress. It is also interactive in that it allows low-progress readers regular access to one-to-one interaction with supportive tutors. These tutors delay any response to reader errors and then respond selectively by supplying the most appropriate type of prompt, contingent on the type of error made by the reader. Tutors rarely tell the reader the correct word. In this way the reader has some control over the nature of the tutoring interaction. The context is social in that tutors use a great deal of specific praise to reinforce readers for using the particular strategies cued by the different types of prompt. The Pause, Prompt and Praise context also facilitates reciprocal skill learning between low-progress readers and tutors. Readers learn to use specific problem-solving skills, and tutors learn to use specific tutoring skills. Mutual gains in skill, as seen in changes in both reader behaviour and tutor behaviour, serve to maintain both the responsive (or interactive) and the social aspects of the learning context, so often lacking in remedial reading.

In this chapter, we have shown how a behavioural interactionist perspective can generate a range of different strategies for helping children learn to read. Young beginning readers may be helped by careful selection of suitable reading materials: natural language texts at an appropriate level of difficulty. These and other antecedents such as the teacher or tutor discussing the story with the reader before oral reading begins have an important influence on children's reading accuracy and self-correction strategies. Children also benefit from increased opportunities to practise sustained silent reading. Teacher modelling, as demonstrated in the USSR studies, increases childrens' participation in recreational reading. These strategies, together with the opportunity to read aloud regularly to a supportive tutor, will be sufficient for most children to learn independent reading skills. For those children who experience difficulty in learning to read, more intensive and interactive remedial reading procedures may be necessary. For some, additional 'practice reading' with a teacher, parent or peer may be sufficient to improve their reading skills. But for others, who experience severe difficulties, more precise and systematic tutoring will be necessary. Pause, Prompt and Praise tutoring by parents and peers has been shown to be particularly effective. In the following chapter we will show how a behavioural interactionist perspective can generate similar strategies for improving children's written and oral language skills.

9

Responsive Contexts for Learning Oral and Written Language

When a person moves to a new country and needs to learn a new language, local people are usually very supportive of hesitating first attempts and are very tolerant of inaccuracies. Fortunately, they typically do not comment on and immediately correct every error which occurs. Rather, it seems that they respond to what they perceive as the speaker's intended message. Even a poorly structured inaccurate request for directions is frequently responded to, with the speaker obtaining at least some of the information required. Similarly, as we have noted earlier, when a young child is learning to speak, parents typically go out of their way to interpret the message the child is trying to communicate, and respond in terms of that message. For example, they may provide an answer to a question, or supply a requested object. Parents clearly do not demand complete accuracy of pronunciation and language structure from the children before responding to their messages. Language does not have to be completely accurate in order to be functional. Given sufficient opportunity to practise using language within a responsive social context with more competent speakers, young children and strangers in a new country receive sufficient natural reinforcement that their language becomes both increasingly fluent and accurate. Unfortunately much of the academic learning which takes place in classrooms is not organized on these principles.

In this chapter we will now turn to focus on oral and written language. We will consider how a behavioural interactionist perspective can help us to organize and develop responsive social contexts in which learning of effective oral and written language skills can take place.

LANGUAGE

In recent years, language research and theory has moved away from viewing language as an innate and inevitable developmental process. In the sixties and early seventies, influenced by the linguist Noam Chomsky, psychologists and educators attempted to explain children's language performance by recourse to inbuilt mechanisms. Contemporary developmental psychologists studying children's language are now much more concerned with explaining children's language learning in terms of the quality of the social contexts in which children interact with adults. In some respects, we see this development as a return to the model of language learning first proposed by B. F. Skinner in his seminal book *Verbal Behavior* (Skinner, 1957). Skinner's work on language was prematurely dismissed, yet it has a subtlety and sophistication which has yet to be fully appreciated by educators. Unfortunately, many naïve behavioural language training strategies have been devised more from clumsy extrapolations from general operant psychology than from an appreciation of language as verbal behaviour.

A behavioural interactionist approach to language learning encompasses the language learner, the language environment (since we know behaviour does not occur in a vacuum) and the language 'teacher'. Such an approach must clarify the functional and contingent relationships between adult and child language in conversations. It must also consider the role of various aspects of the language environment as setting events influencing language behaviour. These include the task or activity the child is engaged in, the presence of and type of stimulus materials and the context or situation.

Sadly, most behavioural language training programmes to date have been highly structured, scripted, adult-controlled sequences which are largely reliant on the model–imitate–reinforce sequence as a teaching methodology. An obvious example is the Distar (Direct Instruction) language programme. Although some limited success can be claimed, particularly with children who are low achieving, most of these programmes show poor evidence of generalization of the new repertoire to the wider environment, (Kiernan, 1984).

The technology of Direct Instruction (Englemann and Carnine, 1982) was adopted by many educational psychologists with great enthusiasm. It involves the use of carefully structured and tightly sequenced teaching materials, presented in a standardardized and unvarying format. Since the programme is fixed, there are minimal opportunities for teacher behaviour to change in response to child behaviour. Uncritical espousal of Direct Instruction by some educationists is a cause for concern particularly where its principles are introduced into educational settings which are radically different from those in which it was developed in the United States.

Many of the studies carried out in the UK attempting to evaluate the effectiveness of Direct Instruction programmes were poorly designed. In many studies, control groups were not included, and where they were, the children did not receive any alternative form of innovative instruction. In our studies carried out at the Centre for Child Study, Distar Language One was compared with alternative, novel programmes. Measurable gains were shown to have occurred following programme training but the gains made by the Distar groups were not superior to those made by children participating in the alternative novel programmes (Wheldall and Wheldall, 1984).

'Motherese'

A well-documented body of research is now available describing the general characteristics of adult language addressed to young language learners, often referred to as 'motherese'. This research suggests probable functions of adult language in facilitating child language learning (Snow and Ferguson, 1977; Colmar and Wheldall, 1985).

The first major function of adult language is the cueing, directing and maintaining of children's attention. This serves as a key prerequisite to successful communication and to more specific language-interactions. Adults speak slowly (at about two-thirds normal adult rate) to children between 18 months and 24 months old. They use more object names, exaggerate and vary intonation patterns, repeat themselves much more often and speak at a higher pitch (see Shute and Wheldall, 1989 for a review of work on vocal pitch and preliminary findings from a sample of British women). Many adults would not be aware that these behaviours are actually components of skilful language teaching. These specific behaviours are a 'natural' response to children's language in order to gain and maintain the child's attention during the conversation. Thus already we can point to the importance of responsive interactive contexts, in which both children and adults learn new skills.

The second major function of the special speech adults use when speaking to young language learners is the presentation of a a simplified language model. This probably facilitates children's comprehension. As the young child does not yet understand adult language, more complex conversations and language-interactions cannot take place. Hence, adults simplify their speech in a number of ways. The resulting simplified language model is, in fact, far better suited to assisting young children to learn to speak.

The simplified language model can be described as having: fewer multi-clause sentences, greater fluency and grammaticality, a significantly shorter mean length of utterance (MLU), a significantly higher proportion of content words over function words and more consistent patterns of word order. It is generally noted that adult MLU (when speaking to children) is almost always slightly greater than the child's MLU. This suggests that the adult presents a language model to the child which is less complex than adult language but also slightly in advance of the child's own level of language skill. McNaughton and Colmar analysed the MLUs of four mothers and their language-delayed children based on samples of natural language data. They found that adult MLU was clearly and consistently shown to be about two or three words longer than the child's MLU (see Colmar and Wheldall, 1985).

In the simplified language model, conversational topics are usually focused around subjects of interest to the young child), and hence are less varied and more related to immediate events. Also, vocabulary is more concrete, more redundant and highly repetitive not only of words but also of familiar sentence frames. The routine repetitiveness of early language interactions between parents and young children is important in providing the child with many opportunities to hear and practise familiar sequences and variations on these sequences. For example, the familiar sentence frame of pronoun, an auxiliary verb and a label is used over and over again. "What's dat?' asks the child. "It is a rabbit', "It is a bus', "It is a blue truck', replies the parent. These examples clearly illustrate the importance of adults responding to children's initiations, and not simply asking questions and giving directions. Conversational interactions require a sharing of control over initiations and changes of topic.

Many early behavioural language programmes have drawn on this type of everyday example. Unfortunately, they have then structured and scripted the language interaction so as to be totally adult controlled and not a response to children's initiations of conversations or to children's continuing attention and interest in an object or event. It is hardly surprising, then, that so much of the effort of typical behavioural language programmes has gone into developing structured methods to capture and maintain child attention. This has led to an emphasis on language as a medium for compliance with adult instruction and responding to adult directions, and a neglect of language as a two-way communication and exchange of information about everyday events.

Some behavioural programmes are also guilty of ignoring the many available opportunities for language teaching in everyday contexts and routines. For example, most language learners either ask for or are given a drink at least four times a day. This is an ideal opportunity for a natural language interaction to occur. Similarly, the average infant has about 2000 nappy changes before toilet training is achieved! In these examples, opportunities are available not only for the repetitive presentation and practice of familiar conversational sequences, but also for the gradual introduction of new input and shared language into the routine, particularly as the child's language repertoire increases.

Descriptive studies have now clarified that a conversation between an adult and child, focused on a topic of joint interest, is the setting in which a young child learns to speak (Bruner, 1975a and b). It provides the child with the opportunity to practise his or her own speech in a familiar context, to learn about turn-taking in conversations (i.e. when to talk and when to listen), to learn new vocabulary and sequences in familiar contexts, to learn how to listen and to hear a lot of simplified and personally relevant adult speech. In many respects, this conversational context constitutes the type of responsive social context we outlined in chapter 7. No conclusive evidence of the usefulness or necessity of these variables can be reached at present. However, they are repeatedly documented in descriptive studies which suggests that they may be important components of effective language learning environments. Wells's study in Bristol provided support for the view that 'children's rate of linguistic development is associated with the quality of the conversation that they experience with adults' (Wells, 1984).

We have noted that this current emphasis on adult–child interactions in child language learning takes us, in large part, back to the model of language learning proposed by Skinner in *Verbal Behavior*. In other words, this more cognitively oriented, developmental perspective, with its focus on the important role of interactions between parent and child in child language development, is congruent with the behavioural view of functional contingencies between the language repertoires of parent and child. Sadly, early applied behavioural technicians preferred to draw more directly on general learning theory derived from laboratory experimental psychology relying heavily on the three-step sequence: adult model – child imitate – adult reinforce. They ignored the potential in the evidence on language learning and teaching observed in natural conversations. The language teaching programmes they developed proved inadequate, in that children's language learned from the model – imitate – reinforce sequence failed to generalize into the natural environment. That is, in their everyday interactions outside the teaching programme, children did not use the specific language they were taught. Researchers are now acutely aware that the more narrow and tightly-controlled and artificial the teaching context, the less likely the behaviour is to generalize to the natural environment.

Setting Events

A behavioural interactionist approach to language learning takes into account the role of setting events and relevant ecological variables. However, antecedent events like the nature of the task, stimulus materials and responsive social contexts have received minimal attention from language researchers. As we have shown in the case of oral reading, setting events can be a major influence on the number and type of language-interactions which occur. Snow (1977) argues that the nature of the activity, rather than the level of difficulty of the activity, is a major influence on parental speech in conversation with young children. By increasing the number of opportunities for conversations between adult and child, the number of available opportunities for language learning and for both parents and children to gain in skill is increased. The work of the Living Environments Group at Kansas University led by Todd Risley (1977) has shown, for example, that assigning staff in a daycare setting to areas (or zones) such that they work with children on a specific activity ensures more contact and thus potentially a greater number of opportunities for adult–child interaction. Risley arranged the structuring of the physical environment to minimize the effort needed by staff to provide physical care, so that staff would be far more available for interaction with children. Thus by 'setting' the conditions in an optimal manner, the probability of conversational interactions (and hence of language learning) is increased.

Another example of the probable effect of a setting variable is the use of books in adult conversational interactions with young language learners. Books provide an immediate opportunity for adults and children to engage in a shared activity which generates two-way language interactions. We have found initial reading books to provide a very supportive context for shared learning and oral language interaction between mothers and children of refugee families learning English as a second language (Glynn and Glynn, 1986). Moerk (1974) comments on the role of books in providing descriptions of the child's world that are simpler than, but functionally parallel to, those in the physical environment.

A study by Baker, Foley, Glynn and McNaughton (1983) investigated two setting events which markedly influence the amount of language used by a group of pre-school children in a daycare setting. This study showed that children initiated more language, and were engaged in more language altogether, under conditions where daycare staff sat at the table, engaged them in conversation and allowed them to serve their own food. Children's language decreased under conditions where daycare staff stood and supervised from a distance and pre-served all the food. The availability and proximity of the supervisors and children serving their own food appeared to operate as powerful setting events for child-initiated language.

Incidental Teaching

This concern with the importance of adult–child interactions in the natural environment and with specifying the appropriate setting events for language-interaction brings us logically to the general model of 'Incidental Teaching' developed by Hart and Risley (1978). Incidental Teaching is predicated upon child initiations and requires the interacting adult to respond to children's initiations by prompting or modelling a slightly more elaborate or complex language form than the child initially produced. By capitalizing on the child's initiation the adult is assured of the child's attention. The child is then encouraged to try to imitate the elaborated response and the adult reinforces the child's language use by providing a required item, giving information or assisting with a task. Let us look at this again in a more concrete form.

In the Incidental Teaching model, the adult's first task is to arrange the learning environment in such a way as to maximize the opportunities for children to initiate language. This may involve, for example, providing a range of attractive play materials, but placing them just beyond children's reach. To obtain a toy, children need to attract adult attention and indicate which toy they want. This necessitates some form of language-initiation. The adult's next task is to respond to these initiations by supplying the child with the object, toy, or help indicated. Skilful teachers may use the opportunity provided by the child's initiation to prompt for a slightly more extended or more elaborate utterance before supplying the desired object or help. In this way children's use of language is reinforced by the very natural process of obtaining what one has requested. The powerful context of an environment with attractive materials and responsive adults provides rich opportunities for children to initiate potential topics of conversation, and for adults to briefly extend those conversations. This procedure has been found highly effective with disadvantaged pre-schoolers by Hart and Risley (1978; 1980), with children who have delayed language and in multi-cultural contexts where children are learning English as a second language, as several of our studies in Birmingham pre-school settings show.

In our first case study (Dolley and Wheldall, 1987) carried out in the Centre for Child Study Nursery Class, the class teacher was introduced to and instructed in the use of Incidental Teaching procedures designed to encourage child-initiated language-interaction. Instruction took the form of oral and written explanation, formal exposition and informal discussion. In addition, samples of teacher–child language interactions were used as examples of the technique operating in the natural classroom environment. Teacher–child language interactions were sampled using a radio-microphone throughout the study and the teacher's responses to child initiations were recorded together with all child initiations addressed to the teacher. After the training session was introduced, the teacher's use of Incidental Teaching procedures increased markedly. As a result, the children initiated more often and fewer of their initiations were ignored by the teacher. During a second intervention the strategy was targeted on a group of four children who had previously made few initiations. The frequency of Incidental Teaching sequences involving this group increased considerably as a result.

We then went on to replicate this small case study using a more rigorous experimental design to demonstrate the effectiveness of Incidental Teaching in increasing the occurrence of child-initiated language-sequences and also to demonstrate that the technique could be successfully applied with second-language learners in a multi-ethnic nursery environment (Dolley and Wheldall, 1988). This study also involved changing the setting events so that access to materials was made contingent upon the child requesting appropriately.

To this end, two nursery class teachers were introduced to and instructed in the use of Incidental Teaching procedures. Both nursery classes included a large proportion of children from Punjabi-speaking homes. Throughout the study teacher–child language-interactions were again sampled using radio microphones and all child initiations were transcribed together with all teachers' responses to child initiations. A multiple baseline design across teachers/classes was employed so that the introduction of Incidental Teaching procedures was staggered following the collection of baseline data, as was the introduction of an amended strategy.

After the initial training session, both teachers' use of Incidental Teaching procedures increased markedly and in both classes children initiated language-interactions more frequently. The total number of words spoken to the teacher and the average number of words spoken per child increased in both groups. During a second phase (the amended strategy), when the teachers arranged the environment so that children were required to request access to certain materials, both the number of child initiations and the teachers' use of Incidental Teaching procedures continued to rise in both classes. In class A, both the total number of words spoken and the average number of words used per child continued to rise. In class B, however, the total number of words spoken and the average number of words used per child fell; but this was because more children with restricted language were becoming involved in language interactions for the first time.

Dolley, Glynn and Wheldall (1988) subsequently carried out a similar study in a New Zealand pre-school setting. A kindergarten teacher was instructed in the use of Incidental Teaching procedures and was asked to arrange her classroom so that children were required to request access to certain materials. Again, the teacher wore a radio microphone during the sessions so that all child language addressed to the teacher, together with all teacher responses, could be accurately recorded. A simple ABA design was employed. After the implementation of the procedures both the number of child initiations and the teacher's use of Incidental Teaching procedures increased markedly. The number of words spoken by the children to the teacher increased considerably and declined when the intervention was withdrawn.

This series of studies thus provides clear evidence for the effectiveness of Incidental Teaching procedures in increasing adult–child language interactions. A number of variations on ways of responding to child-initiated conversations other than those specified in the Hart and Risley (1980) procedure are also available. These include clarifying, interpreting, eliciting and providing feedback, and are all intended to encourage more and more complex language responses in children. However, these variations have not been so extensively researched as the Incidental Teaching procedure. It is also important to note that language itself, in the form of responsive feedback from an adult whether as an acknowledgement, an informative reply, or a comment which extends the conversation, can itself become reinforcing. Children may come to enjoy conversations because they are allowed to share control over the topics of the conversation and to have some direct impact on the behaviour of the adult. Conversation qualifies as a responsive social context; merely responding to adult questions and instructions does not.

Practical Implications

There are a number of implications for the behaviour of teachers who wish to apply a behavioural interactionist perspective to language learning. First, the teacher has an important role in preparing for appropriate conversational interactions. Obviously this includes careful planning of setting events so that a conversational opportunity of interest to the child is made available. This links in with the use of the Incidental Teaching model in which the environment is structured so that the child must speak in order to gain access to appropriate reinforcers. In addition to this, however, the importance is stressed of adults sharing activities with the child, making time to spend with the child and just being available. Quite simply, for a conversation to occur between adult and child, the adult (at a minimum) needs to be present, to be alert and observant and (ideally) to be involved with the child's activity in order to capitalize on any child initiations which may occur (Hart and Risley, 1980). Athough there are no clear data on this, it is evident that the number of language-interactions which occur will be directly related to the amount of contact time between adult and child. What is clear from the data, however, is that Incidental Teaching leads to increased use of language by children, which generalizes to other adults and settings. Hart and Risley's data established that increased language use is closely associated with increased elaboration and complexity. The more we speak, the more skilled we become.

Another technique for language teaching which has emerged from the descriptive literature on adult language addressed to children is adult-initiated sequences. These interactions may be less helpful for child language learning, as 'the most important aspect of the incidental teaching process appeared to be that the child initiated the teaching moment. The child chose the topic and named the reinforcer which his language would function to obtain' (Hart and Risley, 1978). However, there are many instances where adult-initiated conversations may be needed, particularly in directing and organizing child activities and behaviour. Adult-initiated sequences which deliberately encourage child participation may well be useful in instances where child initiations are very infrequent. An adult who carefully prepares the setting, who spends time and engages in activities with the child, may well find that this increases child initiations. However, if it does not, then appropriate adult-initiated sequences, but in the context of child activity and attentional focus, may be more helpful than doing nothing.

One of our studies in a New Zealand childcare setting (Charles, Glynn and McNaughton, 1984) compared the effects of training two childcare workers to use both Incidental Teaching and 'Talking Up' (an adult-initiated procedure). This latter procedure required adults to comment directly and to ask questions about the task or activity the child was engaged in. We found that although the staff readily learned to use both procedures, the Talking Up procedure led to decreases in children's language-initiations. During phases when the staff were asked to increase their use of Talking Up, they had less time available for responding to children's initiations, and children were so busy responding to adult initiations that they had fewer opportunities to initiate language themselves. The context was more a controlling directive one than a responsive social one.

The various procedures described above form the basis for a parental language booklet *Supertalkers: helping your child learn to talk* (Colmar and Wheldall, 1987). The booklet presents simple and clear guidelines for average parents to use in their conversations with their young children. The behavioural interactionist perspective has also proved helpful in running groups and courses for parents of children with language difficulties and for childcare and pre-school staff. We make every effort to assure parents and teachers of the importance of the time they spend with their young children and of the importance of how they interact when they are together. Such courses emphasize *how* you teach language in the pre-school environment rather than *what* you teach, since children themselves will define the content and focus of many conversations in terms of their current interest and activity.

We now return to the more general issues raised. We would not want to be accused of throwing the baby out with the bathwater and so we would emphasize that we still believe that there may be a place initially for structured behavioural language programmes with certain individuals who may be so disabled that they cannot interact with the natural language environment. Children whom Lovaas (1977) described as 'psychotic', for example, may be unlikely to benefit readily from the language interactions in their natural environment, since their so-called 'autistic' features characterize their disability, i.e. they avoid eye gaze, social contact and so on.

However, we do challenge the concept of language as a set of skills amenable to being broken down into a series of behavioural objectives. Perhaps of all human behaviours, language is least amenable to this type of simplistic analysis. Language is embedded within and inseparable from our existence as social beings. Social interaction is what makes us human, and the motivation to be part of our essentially verbal culture is what promotes the rapid learning of language. Babies learn language so quickly because it is critical to successful participation in human culture.

It seems to us that the behavioural objectives model is inappropriate for language learning. Unlike maths or reading, for example, language is effectively modelled and promoted in all its richness and diversity in the natural environment and is available to children, in some form, from birth. Moreover research evidence shows that parents carefully structure the language they direct to their children in a skilful and well-regulated way conducive to rapid language learning. In effect, the natural social environment (including parents as the major influence) teaches children language much more intensively and with much greater success than teachers teach children maths and reading.

Given this perspective, it is questionable to attempt to teach language in isolation from the natural environment which promotes it. Pointing to a picture of a bun with a rissole inside it and saying 'a hamburger' will not teach 'hamburger' as well as a natural situation where a child gets a hamburger (or avoids a hamburger) by saying 'hamburger' (or 'no hamburger') when in the context of the local fast-food outlet. Language facilitation arising naturally in the everyday environment in response to the child's initiations and demonstrations of interest in specific activities and objects is likely to be much more effective because it is more reinforcing to the child. Children get what they want, whether it is a hamburger, a reply, information, attention, more conversation, approval, affection, love or whatever. Brown and Hanlon (1970) were right to use their experimental research to demonstrate that children are rarely praised for the grammaticality of their utterances (they are more likely to be praised for the truth-value of what they say). But they were wrong to attempt to write off behavioural explanations of language learning on the basis of this. A behavioural interactionist perspective does not claim that language is learned only by praise or being told that you are right. (But it is true that some so-called behavioural language intervention programmes appear to assume this.)

In this section we have demonstrated that a behavioural interactionist approach to language can profit from the data base provided by the literature on parent language addressed to children. Moreover, it allows us to formulate specific hypotheses about the role of key variables in child language learning. Behavioural methodology also provides a means for evaluating the effectiveness of specific procedures commonly found in the natural language environment. If we isolate and describe the variables in this way, we may then be in the position of providing a descriptive behavioural explanation of early language learning which has clear implications for language facilitation in responsive social contexts with both 'normal' and language-delayed-children.

WRITING

Many of the principles behind the provision of responsive social contexts for oral language also apply to responsive social contexts for written expression, as we shall see in this section. Nevertheless, some school writing programmes require children to spend many months of instruction in activities such as tracing or forming individual letters, and tracing or copying words, before they are permitted to generate their own writing. Schools provide surprisingly few opportunities for children to engage in expressive writing, and also provide few opportunities for children to see adults modelling academic skills such as writing. Teachers might better serve the acquisition of expressive writing by creating responsive contexts which assist children to write purposefully.

In providing a responsive social context for expressive or communicative writing, it is important to appreciate the notion of a responsive audience. Vargas (1978) has stressed the importance of writing having some observable impact upon an audience. For beginning writers, Vargas goes as far as having young children perform actions and carry out instructions written by the writer. In this way, the beginning writer can 'see' that what is written has some visible effect upon the reader. Such writing is clearly functional and provides the young writer with another set of skills for operating on the environment. For older writers, having such direct and tangible impact on the reader might not be necessary. Instead, the reader might respond with an interested comment, a reaction or an exchange of information. Again, the reader is providing evidence to the writer that the writing has had some effect. For beginning writers, such audience responsiveness should be immediate and frequent, in the same way that parents provide a responsive audience for their young children learning to speak.

However, in a responsive social context, reader responses should never take the form of corrective feedback. Many teachers may be responding to accuracy in children's early writing at the expense of fluency. In providing excessive feedback on the accuracy of letter formation, spelling and syntax, teachers may run the risk of extinguishing fluent communication of ideas and information. This argument is similar to the argument that the vast majority of parents who provide a successful responsive context in which their children learn to speak do not rely on corrective feedback to achieve this. As we noted in the prevous section, Brown and Hanlon (1970) found from direct observation of parent–child interaction that parents responded to the context of their children's speech and not to its form.

This takes us back to our earlier example, of the newly arrived immigrant having to learn the language of a new country. Fortunately, the first hesitant attempts to communicate are responded to by the community in terms of their content or information. Simple instructions and basic requests are usually met, irrespective of the accuracy of the utterance. However, if the community typically responded with corrective feedback, by pointing out inaccuracies in punctuation and grammar, and ignored the content of the language, the newly arrived immigrant would be unlikely to become a fluent speaker. Yet some teachers and adults respond to children's first attempts at writing in just this fashion. Spelling errors, punctuation errors and grammatical errors are marked and commented on. Furthermore, this is often done in a distant, impersonal way, from the perspective of an evaluation by a highly competent performer. This is a far cry from seeing writing as a reciprocal social process.

Some parents, in the home setting, manage to provide powerful, responsive social contexts for their children's early writing. There is both sharing and reciprocation when a parent responds to a child's initiative or request to write by sitting down with the child and 'reading' with real interest what the child is attempting to express.

The content or topic of the writing is shared between the writer and the reader; and by writing more and trying to communicate more ideas, the child is learning another powerful means of gaining and maintaining parental attention.

To the extent that obtaining meaning from what is written is important to both child and parent, the writing task is truly a shared one. To the extent that with time the child becomes more skilled at writing and the parent becomes more skilled at interpreting what is written, the task clearly promotes reciprocal influence. Both parties are modifying the behaviour of the other. To the extent that the setting and the task are positive and enjoyable for both and that the parent avoids corrective feedback on the form of the writing, the essential *social* character of the learning context is preserved.

In these responsive social contexts children can become surprisingly fluent in written communication. Some of our recent studies carried out in New Zealand have been researching this topic. One of our students, Arndt, compared the amount and the accuracy of her seven-year-old daughter's writing at home and at school. The girl wrote consistently more in the same ten-minute period at home than she did at school, although the accuracy of her writing was similar in the two settings. Arndt then began (at home) a strategy of discussing with her child ideas for story-writing and interesting words that might be used. She also began, immediately after the writing was finished, to make personalized comments which responded to the content and ideas in the story. She made no comments on the amount written or on the accuracy of the writing. Results showed that there was a marked increase in the amount written in the writing time and, more importantly, an increase in the accuracy of what was written. Now both the amount and the accuracy of this girl's writing at home surpassed that of her writing at school. The difference can be understood in terms of the differences between the contexts in which the writing took place. The home context had the properties of a responsive social context, while the school context did not. One explanation for the unexpected gains in accuracy in a setting which seemed to promote only fluency is the rewarding sense of competence that results from seeing the effect you can have on your audience. With the greatly increased amount of writing achieved when a responsive audience is available and with writing being an enjoyable social process, becoming more competent and more skilled can be highly reinforcing. Clay (1979) argued that the power of being able to make one's own statement, and of getting better and better at it, is rewarding in itself.

As we have already noted, another important characteristic of a responsive learning context is that it should promote initiations by the learner. The practice in some infant classes of allowing children to try to write their own story beneath a picture they have produced, even though they have not yet mastered all the letters of the alphabet, certainly allows children important initiative in making their own statements. The teacher's response to the content of that statement is every bit as important as providing a written model for the child to copy. It is critical that the demands of the task of making an accurate match of the teacher's model do not outweigh those of trying to generate one's own statement. However, the practice in some junior and middle primary classes of allocating almost all of the available writing time to copying teachers' models and practising handwriting seems to be counter-productive.

If it is true that accuracy of handwriting will improve with fluent practice, and if fluency depends on a responsive social (non-corrective) audience, children might as well generate their own written statements from the outset. In another of our New Zealand studies, carried out in a special class setting (Glynn, McNaughton and Wotherspoon, 1974), children were spending all their writing-time in copying from teacher models. Their teacher believed that they needed first to be completely accurate in forming letters before they could move on to writing material of their own. We suggested a simple strategy which required these children to generate some words and sentences of their own and which reinforced all attempts irrespective of accuracy. The children began to write words and sentences for the first time and, over time, their sentences increased in complexity. Independent raters commented that the children's handwriting was more accurate when they were generating their own sentences than when they were copying the teacher model.

There have been several research studies which have established that reinforcing the amount of writing, and so increasing children's rate of writing, does not result in reductions in accuracy, and can even result in the writing being judged more creative or imaginative or of higher quality (Brigham, Graubard and Stans, 1972; Maloney and Hopkins, 1973). In one of our own studies (Ballard and Glynn, 1975), two independent raters found that stories written under conditions of reinforcement for using more action words were rated of higher quality than stories written under conditions of reinforcement for using more descriptive words. In a later study (Scriven and Glynn, 1983), we provided underachieving fourth-form writers with increased feedback on their writing. We provided daily feedback on rate of writing task completion and only weekly feedback on accuracy. This yielded dramatic gains in the amount of written work completed and smaller gains in accuracy, even though the children's accuracy was already quite high.

The importance of using reinforcement selectively to increase independent behaviour is further illustrated in another of our studies (Wilson and Glynn, 1983). In this study, mildly handicapped children experienced reinforcement for self-generated words and sentences. The programme greatly increased the amount written by these children, to the point where they were maximizing reinforcement for themselves by calling upon the teacher to supply them with the words they wanted (a dependent behaviour), rather than first checking whether the required word was displayed on available wall charts or in personal word lists. As this increase in teacher-dependent behaviour meant the teacher was literally 'run off her feet' supplying children with words, a mild response-cost procedure was introduced to counter some of the unnecessary reinforcing of dependent behaviour. Children now lost a point if the word they asked the teacher to supply was found to be on the wall charts or in personal lists. The teacher continued to supply genuinely new words. Under these altered conditions, there was a dramatic increase in the number of words 'found' by the children themselves. Dependent behaviour was successfully countered by the mild response-cost procedure but fluent writing was maintained by the positive reinforcement for self-generated words and sentences.

In case it might sound overly mechanistic to place such emphasis on rate of writing and amount written, it is worth mentioning an interesting study by Wallace and Pear (1977). This study reported that a number of highly successful professional writers such as Anthony Trollope, Arnold Bennett, Ernest Hemingway and Irving Wallace all kept meticulous charts showing the amount written daily, weekly and monthly. These charts appeared to serve both as a reinforcer for work accomplished and as a stimulus to keep writing. This study and the previous research suggest that there is a possible relationship between fluency and creativity in writing. Unfortunately, in many classrooms children do not have frequent opportunities to engage in their own writing, and when these do occur they are likely to emphasize accuracy rather than fluency.

Although it is clear that it is more important to emphasize rate than accuracy in establishing expressive and communicative writing, providing external teacher contingencies on rate may not be the most effective way to proceed. It is important to re-examine the notion of a responsive audience in the form of a reader who provides individual, personal responses to the content of a child's writing. Perhaps regular access to such an audience, which allows for the development of a reciprocal relationship between writer and reader, would itself increase the rate of writing achieved?

Such a reciprocal relationship occasionally develops between a child and a relative or close friend who regularly exchange letters. Given a positive relationship between the child and another person, exchanging letters can indeed be a shared task with each writer having some visible effect on the writing of the other. There is not one dominant or controlling partner, as in the case of the demanding adult who writes the child a series of questions requiring set answers. Such writers share little of their own ideas or feelings, but confine their participation to corrective or critical comments on what the child wrote in the previous letter.

In contrast, a responsive reader attends to the messages initiated by the writer and responds by communicating reactions, feelings, new ideas or personal information, such as might happen in a conversation. Such letters give as much as, or more than, they demand. These are sometimes the very letters we want to reply to, no matter how busy we might be. Sometimes we surprise ourselves at how much we write when we respond in this way. These rare, extended reciprocal communications are precious indeed. Is it at all possible that something of this responsive social context for writing could be established at school? Could a class teacher organize a context for writing that allowed for continuous sharing of writing with reciprocal influence so that each party could really affect the writing of the other? Could a teacher establish this responsive context for all members of her class? Individual oral response to the content of children's writing would be restricted because of time; but could a teacher supply individual *written* response to children's writing and what would happen if she did?

We carried out a study to investigate the effect of written content feedback upon the expressive writing of a class of eight-year-old children, over two school terms (Glynn, Jerram and Tuck, 1986; Jerram, Glynn and Tuck, 1988). We assessed the effect of written content feedback without any corrective feedback at all. Written content feedback involved the teacher in reading children's writing from a given session and writing a brief (four to five lines) personal response to what each child had written. As suggested earlier, this written feedback attended to the content of what each child wrote and offered a personal reaction, comment or expression of feeling (e.g. empathy, sympathy). Typically, these statements contained personal information about the teacher's experiences, thoughts and ideas where these were triggered by what the child had written. At no time did this written feedback contain any comment on accuracy, spelling or grammar. Nor did the teacher ever make any oral comment about these features.

To provide a context for writing, the teacher set aside three sessions per week, each of about 15 minutes, in which the children were invited to write but never required to do so. They were free to engage in any other quiet activity. In each session the children were free to select their own writing topic and to decide to continue writing on an existing topic or to begin a new one. The children were also free to write on either factual or imaginative topics. Each was supplied with a personal exercise book for use during this special writing time. Writing for each session began on a new page which was dated.

Following a 16-session baseline phase when children wrote according to the above conditions, the teacher introduced written content feedback. This written feedback continued for nine further sessions, after which it was withdrawn and children reverted to writing under baseline conditions. This withdrawal period lasted for only three sessions, since both the teacher and the children were extremely concerned at the loss of what they had all come to regard as a highly positive and enjoyable experience. The process in which the teacher read what the children had written and devised an individual response for each child, while the children read this personal response and then continued with writing something else for the teacher to read, had begun to be an enjoyable experience for both teacher and children. Nevertheless, from an experimental design point of view, three sessions of withdrawal of treatment provided clear evidence of loss in the amount and quality of writing achieved. Following this three-day period of withdrawal, the teacher reintroduced the content feedback procedure and continued it for a further 20 sessions. The study continued beyond this point with the involvement of some of the parents of the children, acting as a responsive audience at home.

Let us consider the performance of two (representative) children, Phillida and Sarah. First, across the baseline phase there was a tendency for both children to write fewer words – i.e., the setting event of a quiet uninterrupted time to write whatever one liked was not sufficient to support an increasing rate of writing. Second, with the introduction of content feedback from the teacher, there were clear gains in amount written by both children. Third, with the withdrawal of content feedback and return to the second baseline period there was a dramatic drop in the amount written by both children. Fourth, with the re-introduction of content feedback from the teacher, there were again marked increases in amounts written by both children. Fifth, both Phillida and Sarah came to write more continuous stories (i.e. stories which extended over two or more days) under the content feedback conditions, especially during the second content feedback phase. Sixth, over time both children came to write stories that were imaginative rather than factual. The pattern depicted in the session-by-session data for Phillida and Sarah was similar to that for the remaining ten children. Analyses of the data from all 12 children showed highly significant effects for the content feedback procedure.

These data clearly indicate a functional relationship between teacher content feedback and fluency in the writing of these children. However, the qualitative data are even more interesting. Random samples of children's writing from each phase of the study were shown to three different sets of raters, who did not know the identity of the child who wrote any sample. Raters were asked to use a seven-point scale to rate each sample on the basis of interest and quality. The three sets of raters were a group of educators (teachers and school inspectors), a group of parents of children in the study and a group comprising some of the children themselves. No child rater received a sample of his or her own writing. The pattern of qualitiative ratings was the same across all three sets of raters. Stories rated highest in quality were those written under conditions of content feedback, and stories rated lowest in quality were those written under baseline conditions. The phase where stories received the lowest ratings of all was the second baseline or withdrawal phase. Throughout the study, repeated measures were made of the accuracy of children's spelling. Under conditions of content feedback, designed to support fluency, it was expected that children might attempt more adventurous words than during phases without content feedback. Hence, spelling accuracy was assessed in terms of children's spelling of those words appropriate to their individual level in their classroom spelling programme. Results confirmed that children did indeed introduce more adventurous or risky words beyond their current spelling levels during content feedback phases. However, on words within their individual spelling levels, children remained highly accurate, close to 100% throughout the study.

Informally, it can be reported that these children were highly motivated at each session to read what the teacher had written to them and to respond with more writing. The writing books became highly prized and highly personal private possessions. In many ways, the books recorded the development of a growing positive relationship with the teacher as much as they recorded changes in children's writing.

This study supports the effectiveness of employing responsive social contexts as a setting for children to acquire fluent expressive and communicative writing. It appears that the type of context in which children learn to speak, through reciprocal interaction with an adult speaker who acts as a responsive audience, is also a powerful context in which children learn writing skills. In this study, the teacher adopted the role of a responsive interacting audience, and not the role of a controlling or corrective one. Through the provision of individual personal feedback in writing, this teacher was able to provide beginning writers with an effective means of influencing an interested and responsive audience. The changes in rate and quality of children's writing, and the increased sharing of experiences and feelings between teacher and children that resulted from their writing, support our claim that writing can be usefully viewed as both an interactive and a social process.

In this chapter, we have argued that both oral and written language skills are best learned and practised within the context of real social interaction. Oral and written language skills are not acquired in an isolated, formal instructional setting for use at some later time. Speaking and writing are interactive social processes. Our behavioural interactionist perspective has allowed us to put these views into practice and to evaluate their effectiveness for individual children and classes. In the following chapter, we will show how our behavioural interactionist perspective might be applied to make schools more positive and more enjoyable for both teachers and children and, as a consequence, more effective.

10

Conclusion: Schools Can be More Positive

A friend of ours has an aunt who used to belong to an esoteric cult that apparently worshipped triangles. After some years she left the cult, however, because (or so she said) it had been 'taken over by extremists'! We know how she feels. For some time we have experienced a degree of uncertainty regarding the company we keep. The problem is that as advocates of the behavioural interactionist approach we have grave misgivings about what some behavioural psychologists advocate to improve learning in schools. We have articulated these concerns at several points in this book and have attempted to spell out the approach and procedures we do advocate. In this final chapter, we will attempt to show how a thoroughgoing implementation of this perspective may be operationalized in primary and secondary school settings. We sketch out a blueprint for how schools can become more positive. In the following short scenes from everyday school life we have attempted to remind you of some of the key points we have stressed during the course of this book. It is clear to us that schools can be more positive and, as a result, more effective.

In class IVQ at Aspiring High School, Jane is writing to her pen-pal, while Michael and Keith are playing chess. Many are reading and some are just chatting quietly. Class teacher Steve Mathews is going over square roots with Jason and Terry, at their request. The whole class has earned 'time off for good behaviour' and are spending the last 15 minutes of their Friday lesson in a variety of activities. According to Steve, the class now work harder and learn far more in four lessons than they did in five before he began his 'free-time' reward system. Fifteen minutes is a small price to pay and, in any case, it gives Steve time to give special attention to Jason and Terry. At the end of term, Steve is planning to bring in his toasted-sandwich maker to make baked bean sandwiches for his remedial maths group, as a special reward for their hard work and achievement. Last term, he borrowed a horror video to show them; they really enjoyed that!

After lunch, Steve settles down in a corner of the staff room and begins to write a letter to Jason's parents. 'Dear Mr and Mrs Dawson, I am writing to let you know that Jason is really getting on well at school this term. He has put the problems of last term behind him and has worked really hard. He has been absent only once to go to the dentist, which you confirmed in your letter, and he has not failed to complete his homework once. We are very proud of his progress, as I am sure you are. . . .'

On the other side of the staff room, Denise Marshall, deputy head is having a quiet word with Jack Fury.

'We've all been through it, Jack – a difficult class like IIIP can be really stressful. But the more you rant and rave, the worse they will get. You know they try to wind you up, so you should try to change your strategy. Ask Steve about that course he went on last year about behaviour management. He swears by it. Susan Phillips, our educational psychologist, ran the course here on site, with some help from the deputy head at Steady Progress Comprehensive.'

When the bell goes Jack returns to the fray and confronts IIIP head-on.

'Now belt up you lot or you're for it. The next one who speaks gets detention. Right that's you Richardson, and you Smith, and Coalport – oh this is ridiculous. . . .'

Steve on the other hand is filling in for a sick colleague with IIS.

'OK then, settle down. As you know, Mrs Beaumont has bronchitis and won't be back until after the holidays, so I'll be taking you. Now before we go any further let's get one or two things clear. Those of you who had me for maths last year will remember that I like to make up a few rules to make life easier for all of us. Would anyone like to suggest a rule for us . . . . Yes, Kim isn't it?'

'"No talking" sir.'

'Thanks Kim, but just call me Mr Matthews – the Queen hasn't knighted me yet! "No talking": What do you think of that, Eric?'

'Mr Matthews, last year you said we could talk quietly if it was about our work.'

'That's right, we don't need total silence. So what do you suggest Eric?'

'How about, "We try to get on with our own work quietly?"'

'Sounds good to me, what do the rest of you think?. . . .Good, everyone agrees. What about another rule? Marsha.'

'"No wandering about the classroom". It puts you off if people keep walking about and interfering.'

'I heard several folk agree with you there Marsha, but let's try and make it more positive, shall we? How about "We stay in our seats when we are working?" OK?'

Later on Steve is quick to spot pupils keeping the rules he had negotiated with the class.

'Yes, Eric, what can I do for you – thanks for putting your hand up, that's one of our rules. . . . Marsha, it was kind of you to let Jane borrow your protractor. . . . I must say this has been a really peaceful lesson – you've allowed each other to get on quietly and it has made my job a lot easier. Keep it up.'

Nor does Steve forget to comment on the quality and quantity of work produced:

'Nigel, you're really getting the hang of these equations now. . . . Marsha, this is neat work. That one's very nearly right. The important thing is that you recognized what sort of problem it was. Check your calculations. I'm sure it's only a simple adding error.'

He ignores the odd clearly non-work-related comment, but he does not let more serious misbehaviour go unchecked. Spotting trouble in the back row, he walks over and looks Wayne straight in the eye and says quietly but firmly:

'Wayne, that's just not on. We do not spoil other people's work. Get on with your own work and leave Simon alone.'

Wayne pulls a cheeky face, shrugs his shoulders ostentatiously but then begins to work.

'That's a good start Wayne' says Steve, ignoring Wayne's non-verbal behaviour.

Meanwhile, further down the road at Great Oaks Primary, Molly Evans is reading the latest Ruth Rendell thriller, and she takes pains to let her class see that she is really enjoying her book. The children in her class are following her example and are reading quietly in their daily USSR period. The only sound is the turning over of pages and the occasional cough.

Next door Rob Walker is organizing a play-writing activity. Since the pupils are to work co-operatively to produce scripts, they have quickly and quietly moved their desks from rows to table groups. They can now communicate ideas effectively to each other. Before lunch, they were completing maths exercises and found it easier to concentrate while sitting in rows. Once the groups are settled Rob returns to his desk and begins to write in one of the children's exercise books. 'What a great idea for a story, Miriam. I remember when I got lost in a snowstorm once – it was very frightening. My dad had to come and look for me. I wonder who will rescue Polly and Peter – I'm looking forward to reading what happens next.'

Next day, Miriam collects her exercise book from the shelf at the front of the room. Rob Walker reminds the class:

'Remember, this is our Quiet Writing Time; you can write about anything you like in your exercise books, or if you don't want to write today, you can read quietly by yourself.'

Miriam opens her exercise book to the story she was writing previously. She reads Rob's comments and smiles at the thought of Rob Walker in a snowstorm. Fancy *him* being frightened! She begins writing, fairly quickly, trying to picture Rob Walker's surprise when he reads that Polly and Peter ran to shelter in a railway tunnel. . . .

Further down the corridor in the infant reception class, four- and five-year olds are having an art and craft lesson. Diane Derby has supplied each table with paper, brushes and paint. She has kept back drinking straws, glue, glitter and lentils and tells the class that they only need to ask if they would like to use these extra materials. She is particularly anxious to encourage more language use from children from non-English speaking homes. After a few minutes, a little boy comes shyly forward. Chris smiles encouragingly and waits for him to speak, knowing that his English is still very limited.

'Teacher . . . . blow' he says, simply pointing to the drinking straws on Chris's desk.

'You want to blow your paint with a straw, Marco? Here you are – here's a straw. Can you say that, "straw please".'

'Staw pease.'

'That's super, Marco – take your straw and blow your paint to make a picture.'

She touches Marco lightly on the shoulder and smiles again. Marco returns happily to his seat clutching his straw.

Back at Aspiring High, a first-form written language lesson is in full swing. Pupils are seated in small groups around tables. They are discussing whether the local radio station broadcasts enough material that is genuinely local in content. There is a great deal of enthusiastic talking. A brief 'ping' sounds from a tape-recorder. Alan Green briefly looks around the room, notices that all members of group two are seated, heads lowered and listening while only one pupil is speaking. He walks over to group two and says 'Very good group two. I like the way you are taking turns to hear what each has to say. And I like the way you're all getting on with your task. Take another point towards your group's free time in the games corner. Keep up the good work.'

In a room nearby, Sarah Hurley, remedial reading teacher at Aspiring High, pulls a small tape recorder out of her bag, and waves it at her colleague Alan.

'I tried it Alan, and I was horrified.'

'Tried what?'

'You know – Susan Phillips's suggestion that we should actually record ourselves hearing a child read. Well, I did. I asked Harriet if she'd read with me from her current reader. She was a bit suspicious but she decided to have a try. So she read on, with me helping out for about five minutes. Then I took the tape home last night and played it back. What a shock! She made about six mistakes and I crashed in on five of them – immediately telling her the right words. And the sixth one she actually corrected herself, but I didn't even notice! Twice I said "No that's not it, you've said that before" and I didn't praise her at all. I sounded really nit-picking.'

'Don't feel so bad about it – that's only five minutes of tape', Alan says reassuringly.

'No, but suppose I'm like that all the time. It's awful. I thought I was much more positive than that!'

'Well, at least you've done the exercise for Susan Phillips – I was too embarrassed.'

'You can't be! If I can risk it, you can! Go on give it a try, I'll line up another of my special readers for you.'

"Go on then, twist my arm – what have I got to lose?'

Back at Great Oaks Primary, David Brown is seated beside Sean who is a ten-year old experiencing reading difficulties. Sean has chosen a story about motor racing from a box of books which David had assembled as being of about the right difficulty for Sean. David and Sean have just been talking about Formula One cars, drivers and some well-known circuits around the world. Now Sean begins to read the first sentence:

'The McLaren m-m-mak. . . .I don't know this word, I can't read it. . . .'

After waiting about five seconds David Brown says "Well, try reading on to the end of the sentence.'

Sean continues, "pulled into the pits for a wheel change.'

'OK' says his teacher, 'what sort of thing would a McLaren be, driving into the pits?'

'A car' replies Sean.

'Yes, that's nearly right, but this is another word for a car – a special technical word. . . .'

'M – ma – machine!' concludes Sean.

'Exactly' says David, 'Now carry on, you're doing fine.'

A few minutes later Sean reads 'The mechanic threw down the power spinner.'

David's eyebrows raise, but he resists saying anything, and waits.

'Oh, *spanner*!' says Sean, 'the word is spanner!'

'That's great. You noticed it wasn't quite right, and you corrected it all by yourself. Excellent.'

Around two weeks after this episode, Sean and his mother are talking with David Brown after school. Sean's mother is delighted to find that Sean is to be moved on to a more difficult reading book, because he is reading his current one at 98 per cent accuracy.

'I am remembering to praise him for working things out for himself' she says, 'and I am remembering to wait when he makes a mistake. . . .'

David Brown responds: 'That's wonderful Mrs Brennan, pausing is the hardest thing of all – but have you noticed that when you pause, Sean might just be able to help himself?'

'Oh yes, he often does now – don't you Sean?'

Sean smiles sheepishly.

'Now Sean,' reminds David Brown, 'remember your mum has got a lot of things to learn in this reading together, not just you. How do you think she is coming on?'

'Well she doesn't keep on and on at me when I forget a word – now she helps me to work it out for myself.'

'Well, that's a terrific start for both of you' adds David, 'but I did want you both to know that it's time for Sean to tackle something a bit harder – he's hardly making any mistakes at all on this material. How about we take down this other box here, and let you choose another book? Remember you'll make a few more mistakes at first, but you'll soon get into it. See which one you'd like.'

Sean beams proudly and seizes hold of yet another motor racing book.

'This is about the Monaco Grand Prix' he explains and he wanders off to flick through the pages.

David Brown says to Sean's mother 'I think you're both coming along very nicely. But let me check out another point with you. Do you remember what you should do if he makes a mistake and that mistake makes no sense at all?'

'Yes, I think so. I should give him a clue about the meaning of the word, from the rest of the story or the picture – and see if he can work it out from there. . . .'

'Yes, that's fine. You really are getting good at this.'

'Yes, that's true, but I'm learning even more about motor racing!'

Susan Phillips, the educational psychologist, is talking with Sarah Hurley over morning coffee in the staffroom at Aspiring High.

'Thanks for letting me spend half an hour in your classroom this morning, Sarah, I thought that lesson went over really well.'

Sarah smiles, 'Is that a reinforcer? – Seriously, how did I do with positive attention? – I tried to catch people being good.'

'You made 27 praise comments to children who were working, or who seemed to have finished their maths, and only five or six reprimands to children who were messing about – and I really liked the way you went over to their seats individually and commented quietly to each one. You've got that technique mastered now. How did you think the lesson went?'

Sarah pauses for a moment and answers: 'Well, I was conscious of you being there, and I did feel just a bit silly when I said to Rebecca "Oh, I do like the way you've got back to your work again", after she'd been turning around with two pencils between her teeth!'

Susan Phillips laughs: 'Oh yes, I saw that too – she did distract quite a few with that display – but did you notice what happened *after* your comment to her? She looked *very* puzzled, and then began working quietly – and so did the two girls behind her – and the one beside her. It's just a case of treating their attending and participation just as seriously and carefully as we treat their academic work. We simply can't take good behaviour for granted.'

'I must say I do feel I'm being more constructive with these pupils – I only hope I can keep it up.'

These short scenes depict a behavioural interactionist perspective in operation in primary and secondary schools. We will now try to relate some of these events to the principles of this perspective, which we introduced in chapter 2. Let us take the principles one by one.

1 *Employs the methods of applied behaviour analysis* We are by no means suggesting that busy teachers should try to become fully-fledged academic researchers, struggling to implement some of the research designs mentioned throughout this book. Far from it. What we are suggesting is that teachers might be a little more aware of the need for gathering objective data, and of making their decisions into data-based decisions. Sarah Hurley at Aspiring High School showed a positive commitment to data-based decisions when she accepted Susan Phillips's challenge to tape-record her interaction while she was hearing reading. She was a little shocked at what she found, but she bravely faced up to the data on her own behaviour, even if it was not quite what she was expecting! She was certainly responsive to the information contained in these data, which is a critical step in monitoring and implementing behaviour change. David Brown, too, responded to his data on Sean's reading progress. Once David found that Sean was reaching 98 per cent accuracy on his current book, he immediately recommended an advancement to a more difficult text.

Alan Green showed his commitment to a behavioural approach by indicating to his three discussion groups to record a point every time the 'ping' signal had caught them on-task. With this record, Alan and all of his class would have a permanent record of their appropriate behaviour from lesson to lesson. This would serve both as a measure of reward (earned time at chosen activities) and as an indicator of how the children's behaviour was changing over time. David Brown's careful use of the Pause, Prompt and Praise procedures would ensure that he obtained a detailed and systematic observation record of Sean's reading strategies and of Mrs Brennan's learning to implement the procedures correctly. Miriam's writing exercise book would also leave Rob Walker a permanent record of Miriam's writing and his written feedback to her, over a long period of time. Susan Phillips had recorded some highly specific data on Sarah Hurley's praise and reprimands from the lesson she agreed to observe for her. Sarah was eager to receive this information, as her interaction with Susan indicates. Sarah and Susan knew exactly what the other meant by praise and reprimands, since they had agreed on a specific definition before Susan began to observe.

2 Recognises the importance of natural settings and contexts

Teachers employing a behavioural interactionist perspective are skilled at structuring their classroom environments so that they will actively promote the learning outcomes they are seeking. Rob Walker made a point of getting his pupils to move their desks from rows into group formations, before assigning them a discussion task. When the time came for them to discuss their local radio station, Rob's class could look at each other, listen to each other and interact independently of Rob himself and of the other groups. David Brown knew Sean so well that he was able to assemble, in advance of Sean's reading session, a set of reading books that were of just the right difficulty for Sean, neither too difficult nor too easy. Sean was thus presented with a task which he could manage but in which he was also able to learn from the errors he made. David also allowed Sean consistently to select books about motor racing. Self-selection of books of the right level of difficulty and about interesting topics proved to be powerful setting events for Sean's progress in reading. Diane Derby recognized the importance of her art and craft lesson as a natural context in which Marco might try to use language. She waited for the naturally occurring opportunity of Marco's request before she required him to improve on his statement. In chapter 8, we reviewed a series of studies showing the very strong effects on children's recreational reading from having their teachers directly model silent reading of their own books. This is a very simple, natural and almost effortless means of increasing children's engagement with reading material. We wonder why the procedure is not also employed within other subject areas, such as expressive writing, painting, drawing and even physical fitness!

3 Strives to maximise the use of naturally occurring reinforcers

We are particularly concerned that teachers employing a behavioural interactionist perspective should get to know their pupils well enough to learn what are the natural reinforcers readily available, or reasonably accessible, in their schools. Complicated token economies are not only unnecessary in the regular school setting but they may get in the way of more naturally occurring and potentially reinforcing interactions between teachers and pupils. Steve Mathews knew that watching horror films was very rewarding for his Aspiring High School fourth-formers. He capitalized on this knowledge, and on access to the school video recorder, and provided an extremely powerful reinforcer for the pupils. His baked bean toasted sandwiches were another masterstroke. These too were a locally popular item, as he knew. But the experience of a *teacher* making the sandwiches, and serving them up for his pupils was a wonderful role reversal, and produced a genuine responsive, social context. We suspect that sharing Steve's company and sharing food with him on an equal footing may have been at least as powerful a reinforcer as the baked bean sandwiches! Steve Mathews also showed his skill at pin-pointing his positive attention in the classroom. In one lesson we saw him accepting Kim's contribution to the class rules, while still seeking further input from other pupils. He delivered positive attention to the whole class at the end of the lesson for their social behaviour by sharing with them his pleasure at how peaceful the lesson had been. He also managed to praise Nigel for his completed academic work, and Marsha for her close attempt at a correct maths answer. Diane Derby utilized the reinforcers already available in her lesson materials when she rewarded Marco for his language initiation and his improved language statement by giving him the straw he had requested. She also used touch, a powerful reinforcer with young children. Alan Green displayed great precision in his use of teacher praise when his class was divided into three groups for discussion. He used his positive attention to keep all groups discussing, with a minimum of interruption. Rob Walker reinforced Miriam's expressive writing in the most natural and appropriate way, by writing a personal response, identifying himself with her story and sharing some of his own experience.

4 *Responds to empirical evidence from non-behavioural theoretical perspectives* Much of the research presented in chapters 8 and 9 on reading, oral language and writing, in our view, clearly exemplifies a behavioural interactionist perspective. However, this research was also designed on the basis of ideas and theories from other academic fields, in particular child development and cognitively oriented theories of the processes involved in reading, writing and speaking.

When Diane Derby successfully applied the Incidental Teaching strategy with Marco, she was applying a strategy that relates very closely to the notion of the primary developmental context, as espoused by the developmental psychologist Urie Bronfenbrenner (1979). The concept of a 'responsive social context', as developed and illustrated throughout this book, is a combination of Bronfenbrenner's perspective and our own emerging perspective. David Brown praised Sean for his self-correction of 'spanner', and he reminded Sean's mother to prompt Sean with a clue about the meaning of the word, if Sean's attempt did not make sense. David was applying a theoretical model which views learning to read as a cognitive task of learning to obtain information from continuous text material, using a wide range of available sources of information. Similarly, the research reported on 'motherese' which identifies natural language teaching strategies comes from mainstream developmental psychology. However, in the examples from Aspiring High School and Great Oaks Primary School, and in all the research cited in this book there is a strong commitment to operationalizing these theories or perspectives in terms of observable behavioural events and interactions.

5 *Emphasises the interactive nature of learning* We have stressed repeatedly the importance of learning interactions having two-way effects. Powerful learning interactions are those which result in gains in skill for both 'teacher' and 'learner'. People enjoy working together on genuinely shared tasks where they both become more skilful. We have noted that parents as well as infants become more and more skilled as a result of learning to communicate with each other through the medium of oral language interactions. We have noted from the studies of peer tutoring of reading that there are typically gains in reading accuracy and comprehension for tutors as well as tutees. This is particularly so when tutors themselves have reading difficulties. Paradoxically, it is not necessarily the best readers, therefore, who will make the best tutors. It seems that powerful learning contexts arise when both parties stand to gain in skill. David Brown at Great Oaks Primary school was very pleased with Sean's progress in reading and his mother's progress at learning the Pause, Prompt and Praise Procedures. He was not at all surprised at Mrs. Brennan's remark '. . . .and I'm learning even more about motor racing!' We believe that schools should do a great deal more to capitalise on the vast and underused educational resource available in parents and peers.

6 *Seeks to assist children to assume a greater degree of control over their own learning* Throughout the book we have also stressed the importance of teachers sharing control over learning interactions with their pupils. Teachers do not and should not initiate *all* the interactions, determine when they should begin and end, and what they should be about. Steve Mathews at Aspiring High negotiated his classroom rules with his pupils. He did not impose them unilaterally. He responded positively to the suggestions from his pupils, and so shared with them some of the responsibility for managing the behaviour in the classroom. Alan Green's use of the tape-recorded 'pings' to cue himself to monitor and praise each group table in his classroom is also a means of introducing his pupils to monitoring and reinforcing their own behaviour. Alan plans to issue each of his pupils with a card which they can tick every time a 'ping' catches them working. He also plans to negotiate with them a set of rewarding activities which they can obtain with their completed cards. Alan and his pupils will be sharing responsibility for the behaviour which occurs in their classroom. Similarly Diane Derby's Incidental Teaching strategy, where she waited for Marco to make a request, provided the opportunity for Marco to initiate language – and to learn to use language to gain some control over his environment.

7 *Focuses on broader educational issues than just schooling* The behavioural interactionist perspective represented by the studies reviewed in this book embodies a view of children's learning that is not limited to the classroom. Strategies for incidental teaching of language are more readily found in home settings and used by parents in their natural interactions with their children. Responsive feedback for children's early attempts at writing is also very effectively used by parents at home. Indeed, we argue that schools should try to incorporate some of these more interactive and responsive contexts into their routines. This raises the issue of a much closer partnership between parents and teachers. Our research has clearly demonstrated the effectiveness of parents as tutors of their own children, even children who are several years behind in their reading. We are also concerned at the ways in which the trappings of schooling can interfere with real education. Teacher-pupil battles about trivia such as dress or hairstyle militate against positive, interactive learning contexts.

8   *Encourages initiations by the learner*   We have noted throughout this book that opportunities to initiate interactions is one of the hallmarks of contexts for independent learning. Children cannot initiate interactions in contexts where teachers are totally involved in issuing questions, instructions and directives and reinforcing compliance with those objectives. Teachers need to find ways of relinquishing some of their direct, supervisory control of children's behaviour in favour of a more responsive style of interaction. Paradoxically, this is not achieved simply by teachers withdrawing into their shells but, as we have seen in chapter 9, it requires teachers actively to structure and prepare the classroom environment so that children's initiations are more likely to occur. Diane Derby carefully prepared her classroom for an art lesson, but strategically withheld some of the materials. Marco needed to take the initiative and ask her for a staw. She was then able to implement a brief Incidental Teaching interaction by requiring just a small improvement in Marco's language before she supplied the straw. Several of our studies have confirmed the effectiveness of this strategy for Incidental Teaching of language in nursery and pre-school settings in the UK and in New Zealand. We also noted that packaged programmes of Direct Instruction procedures concern us greatly because of their lack of opportunities for children to initiate and for teachers to deviate from the standard instructional pattern in order to respond to any initiations from children. One of our own studies (reported in chapter 9), certainly showed that in one daycare setting, when teachers were instructed to increase their use of an adult-initiated strategy to improve children's language, then the number of child initiations of language decreased.

9   *Values the learning opportunities provided by errors*   From our behavioural interactionist perspective, errors are prime sources of information for both teachers and learners. Indeed, we recommend the deliberate provision of reading material sufficiently challenging for some errors to occur. What the reader does and what the tutor does, contingent on an error is crucial for the establishment of a learning context that is positive and interactive, or negative and controlling. We have noted that if teachers regard errors as opportunities for immediate corrective feedback, and for supplying the correct word, readers will have no opportunity to notice that they have made an error or try to correct that error. Extended interactions of this sort will lead to a learning context that reinforces dependency of the learner on teacher support. On the other hand, if

teachers regard oral reading errors as opportunities for children to learn, they will delay or withhold any immediate attention, and wait to see what the learner will do. Learners may self-correct their own errors, in which case the teachers can then provide positive reinforcement for the reader's independence. Even if learners' first attempts at self-correction are unsuccessful, teachers can then supply prompts or clues, to provide further support for learners' attempts to solve their own problems. From the point of view of teachers, errors provide opportunities for monitoring and evaluating their own teaching behaviour. They can assess whether or not the 'help' they provide children is making them more or less dependent. David Brown has learned through his use of the Pause, Prompt and Praise procedures that his pausing for five seconds after Sean's errors is actually giving Sean a chance to correct those errors by himself. David also notices that Sean is getting better and better at 'solving' unknown words from prompts about the context of the story. In short, Sean is becoming more and more independent in his reading, and David is having to prompt him less and less. In a very real sense Sean is beginning to take responsibility for his own reading.

10 *Recognises the complex professional skills required of teachers*
David Brown certainly learned that Sean's mother and he together could combine their resources and help Sean to overcome his reading difficulties. David took on the additional role of sharing his skills with Mrs Brennan, by helping her learn the Pause, Prompt and Praise procedures. In our view, David's role as a teacher is enhanced, not diminished, by his working in partnership with Mrs Brennan. David still retains professional responsibility for monitoring Sean's progress, promoting him to new book levels, and selecting a range of appropriate level reading material. Mrs Brennan now has the skills to maintain and support Sean's learning, in the responsive social context established by David. Other teachers, especially those in the studies of peer tutoring reviewed in Chapter 9, have also taken on additional roles of training peers as tutors of children with reading difficulties. This has *not* been an opting out or a short cut. Rather it has been a case of sharing some of their teaching skills with pupils and establishing learning contexts in which older and younger low-progress readers can interact, and in which the older readers can learn to implement behavioural strategies to promote independent reading. The teachers' role in this process is again enhanced, in our view. They are not simply contributing to children learning through their own teaching skills, but they are harnessing the resources of

the peer group and channelling these resources constructively so that children can help each other learn. Working in partnership with parents, peers and colleagues calls for complex professional skills, such as communicating with adults as well as with children, empowering others to solve their own problems and monitoring the progress of parents or peers in implementing specific teaching procedures.

These skills are not typically included in pre-service teacher education programmes, despite widespread calls for parent–teacher partnerships and community involvement in schools. For the time being at least these skills, along with skills in classroom management and strategies for positive teaching, will need to be acquired through in-service courses such as INSET programmes and through the teacher education programmes offered by educational psychologists or other professionals working with teachers. Many educational psychologists in New Zealand and in the UK are well prepared by their training and experience in aspects of the behavioural interactionist perspective to provide on-site support and leadership for teachers wanting to learn more about the strategies described in this book. Susan Phillips was doing a sound job of helping Sarah Hurley at Aspiring High School to learn to be more selective in her use of reinforcement in her classroom. In the UK and in NZ in-service courses such as BATPACK and BATSAC, aimed at introducing practising teachers, primary and secondary, to more positive approaches to teaching are becoming more readily available. With increased experience in working in partnership with colleagues, parents and peers and in sharing their skills with others, teachers will, in our view, qualify for the title of *educators*.

Over the ten years we have been researching together in the UK and New Zealand, some of our psychologist and teacher colleagues have expressed a great deal of sympathy for the wider behavioural interactionist perspective we have put forward. Some, however, have been surprised to learn that this perspective still qualifies as a 'behavioural' one. Similarly, some behaviourally oriented psychologists may view some of our criticisms of certain aspects of current behavioural practice as a weakening of our resolve or as a "sell out". But we do not view our work as a sell out of behavioural principles. We see our work as addressing a range of contemporary *educational* questions within a behavioural methodology. Much of the earlier behavioural work in education virtually ignored the social contexts and interactive settings in which children and teachers operate. We are not seeking to devalue the importance of contingencies of reinforcement: rather, we are proposing that behaviour analysis will have more to offer education if reinforcement contingencies are understood in terms of how they operate in naturally occurring educational contexts.

Suggestions for Further Reading

Glynn, T. and Wheldall, K. (Eds) (1988). Changing Academic Behaviour. Special double issue of *Educational Psychology*, 8 (1 and 2).

McNaughton, S., Glynn, T. and Robinson, V. (1987). *Pause, Prompt and Praise: effective tutoring for remedial reading*. Birmingham: Positive Products.

Wheldall, K. (ed.) (1987). *The Behaviourist in the Classroom*. London: Allen and Unwin.

Wheldall, K. and Merrett, F. (1984). *Positive Teaching: the behavioural approach*. London: Allen and Unwin.

Wheldall, K., Merrett, F. and Glynn, T. (eds) (1986). *Behaviour Analysis in Educational Psychology*. London: Croom Helm.

References

Allington, R. L. (1980). Teacher interruption behaviours during primary grade oral reading. *Journal of Educational Psychology*, 72, 371–377.

Allington, R. L. (1983). The reading instruction provided readers of differing reading abilities. *The Elementary School Journal*, 5, 548–599.

Axelrod, S., Hall, R. V. and Tams, A. (1979). Comparison of two common classroom seating arrangements. *Academic Therapy*, 15, 29–36.

Baer, D. M., Wolfe, M. M. and Risley, T. R. (1968). Some current dimensions of applied behavior analysis. *Journal of Applied Behavior Analysis*, 1, 91–7.

Baker, M., Foley, M., Glynn, T. and McNaughton, S. (1983). The effect of adult proximity and serving style on pre-schoolers' language and eating behaviour. *Educational Psychology*, 8, 137–48.

Ballard, K. D. and Glynn, T. (1975). Behavioural self-management in story writing with elementary school children. *Journal of Applied Behavior Analysis*, 8, 387–98.

Bandura, A. (1977). *Social Learning Theory*. New Jersey: Prentice-Hall.

Barlow, M. and Hersen, D. H. (1984). *Single Case Experimental Design: strategies for studying behavior change. (2nd ed)* New York: Pergamon.

Becker, W. C., Madsen, C. H., Jnr., Arnold, C. R. and Thomas, D. R. (1967). The contingent use of teacher attention and praise in reading classroom behaviour problems. *Journal of Special Education*, 1, 287–307.

Becker, W. C., Thomas, D. R., and Carnine, D. (1969). *Reducing Behaviour Problems: an operant conditioning guide for teachers.* Urbana, Ill.: National Laboratory on Early Childhood Education.

Bennett, N. and Blundell, D. (1983). Quantity and quality of work in rows and classroom groups. *Educational Psychology*, 3, 93–105.

Bennett, N., Desforges, C., Cockburn, A. and Wilkinson, B. (1984). *The Quality of Pupil Learning Experiences*. London: Lawrence Erlbaum Associates.

Bevan, K. and Wheldall, K. (1985). A touching way to teach. Paper presented to the Annual Conference of the Education Section of the British Psychological Society. (Centre for Child Study, University of Birmingham).

Bijou, S. W. and Baer, D. M. (1978). *Behavior Analysis of Child Development*. New Jersey: Prentice Hall.

Boydell, D. (1974). Teacher–pupil contact in junior classrooms. *British Journal of Educational Psychology*, 44, 313–18.

Boydell, D. (1975). Pupil behaviour in junior classrooms. *British Journal of Educational Psychology*, 45, 122–9.

Brigham, T. A., Graubard, P. S. and Stans, A. (1972). Analysis of the effects of sequential reinforcement contingencies on aspects of composition. *Journal of Applied Behavior Analysis*, 5, 421–9.

Bronfenbrenner, U. (1979). Contexts of child rearing: problems and prospects. *American Psychologist*, 34, 844–50.

Brophy, J. (1981). Teacher praise: a functional analysis. *Review of Educational Research*, 51, 5–32.

Brown, R. and Hanlon, C. (1970). Derivational complexity and order of acquisition in child speech. In J. R. Hayes, (ed.) *Cognition and the Development of Language*. New York: Wiley.

Bruner, J. S. (1975a). From communication to language – a psychological perspective. *Cognition*, 3, 255–87.

Bruner, J. S. (1975b). The ontogenesis of speech acts. *Journal of Child Language*, 2, 1–19.

Burdett, C., Egner, A. and McKenzie, H. (1970). *Report of the Consulting Teacher Program*, Vol. 2. Vermont: University of Nebraska Press.

Charles, H., Glynn, T. and McNaughton, S. (1984). Childcare workers' use of talking up and incidental teaching procedures under standard and self-management staff training packages. *Educational Psychology*, 4, 199–212.

Clay, M. M. (1969). Reading errors and self correction behaviour. *British Journal of Educational Psychology*, 39, 47–56.

Clay, M. M. (1979). *Reading: the patterning of complex behaviour*. (2nd edn). Auckland: Heinemann Educational Books.

Clements, J. E. B. and Tracey, D. B. (1977). Effects of touch and verbal reinforcement on the classroom behaviour of emotionally disturbed boys. *Exceptional Children*, 37, 553–4.

Cohen, D. (1977). *Psychologists on Psychology*. London: Routledge and Kegan Paul.

Colmar, S. and Wheldall, K. (1985). Behavioural language teaching: using the natural environment. *Child Language Teaching and Therapy*, 1, 199–216.

Colmar, S. and Wheldall, K. (1987). *Supertalkers: helping your child learn to talk*. Birmingham: Positive Products.

Dawe, H. C. (1934). The influence of size of kindergarten group upon performance. *Child Development*, 5, 295–303.

Department of Education and Science (1967). *Children and their Primary Schools (Plowden Report)*. London: HMSO.

Department of Education and Science (1975). *A Language for Life* (Bullock Report). London: HMSO.

Dolley, D., Glynn, T. and Wheldall, K. (1989). Increasing preschoolers' language use through incidental teaching. *New Zealand Journal of Educational Studies*, 24 (in press).

Dolley, D. and Wheldall, K. (1987). Talking to teacher – using incidental teaching to encourage child initiations in the nursery classroom: a case study. *Child Language Teaching and Therapy*, 3, 277–92.

Dolley, D. and Wheldall, K. (1988). Developing functional language with young children from English-speaking and Punjabi-speaking home backgrounds: incidental teaching and contingent access to materials. *Educational Psychology*, 8, 101–16.

Engelmann, S. and Carnine, D. W. (1982). *Theory of Instruction*. New York: Irvington.

Farquhar, C. (1987). Little read books. *Times Educational Supplement*, 8 May 1987, p. 25.

Florio-Ruane, S. (1983). What's so hard about writing? *Elementary School Journal*, 84, 93–99.

Frazier, N. and Sadler, M. (1973). *Sexism in School and Society*. London: Harper and Row.

Galton, M., Simon, B. and Croll, P. (1980). *Inside the Primary Classroom*. London: Routledge and Kegan Paul.

Garvey, V. and Hegarty, M (1987). Correlates of leisure-time reading. *Journal of Research in Reading*, 10, 3–20.

Glynn, E. L. and Thomas, J. D. (1974). The effects of cueing on self-control of on-task classroom behavior. *Journal of Applied Behavior Analysis*, 7, 299–306.

Glynn, E. L., Thomas, J. D. and Shee, S. M. (1973). Behavioral self-control of non-task behavior in an elementary class. *Journal of Applied Behavior Analysis*, 6, 163–71.

Glynn, T. (1982). Antecedent control of behaviour in educational contexts. *Educational Psychology*, 2, 215–29.

Glynn, T. (1983). Building an effective teaching environment. In K. Wheldall and R. J. Riding (eds), *Psychological Aspects of Learning and Teaching*. London: Croom Helm.

Glynn, T. (1985). Contexts for independent learning. *Educational Psychology*, 5, 5–15.

Glynn, T. (1987). Contexts for independent learning for children with special needs. *Behavioural Approaches with Children*, 11, 5–19.

Glynn, T. and Glynn, V. (1986). Shared reading by Cambodian mothers and children learning English as a second language: Reciprocal gains. *The Exceptional Child*, 33(3), 159–72.

Glynn, T., Jerram, H. and Tuck, B. (1986). Writing as an interactive social process. *Behavioural Approaches with Children*, 10, 116–26.

Glynn, T. and McNaughton, S. (1985). The Mangere Home and School Remedial Reading Procedures: continuing research on their effectiveness. *New Zealand Journal of Psychology*, 14(2), 66–77.

Glynn, T., McNaughton, S. S., Robinson, V. and Quinn, M. (1979). *Remedial Reading at Home: helping you to help your child.* Wellington: NZCER.

Glynn, T., McNaughton, S. S. and Wotherspoon, A. T. (1974). Modification of reading, writing and attending behaviour in a special class for retarded children. Unpublished paper, Education Department, University of Auckland.

Griffith, C. R. (1921). A comment upon psychology of the audience. *Psychology Monographs*, 30, 36–47.

Gumperz, J. J. and Hernandez-Chavez, E. (1972). Bilingualism, bidialectism and classroom interaction. In C. B. Cazden, V. P. John and D. Hymes (eds), *Functions of Language in the Classroom.* New York: Teachers' College Press.

Hart, B. and Risley, T. R. (1978). Promoting productive language through incidental teaching. *Education and Urban Society*, 10, 407–29.

Hart, B. and Risley, T. R. (1980). In vivo language intervention: unanticipated general effects. *Journal of Applied Behavior Analysis*, 13, 407–32.

Heinig, R. (1976). A descriptive study of teacher–pupil tactile communication in grades 4 through 6. *Dissertations Abstracts International*, 36, 12A, 7948.

Heller, M. S. and White, M. A. (1975). Rates of teacher approval and disapproval to higher and lower ability classes. *Journal of Educational Psychology*, 67, 796–800.

Henderson, W. and Glynn, T. (1986). A feedback procedure for teacher trainees working with parent tutors of reading. *Educational Psychology*, 6, 2, 159–77.

Holt, J. (1969). *How Children Fail.* London: Penguin.

Houghton, S., Merrett, F. and Wheldall, K. (1988). The attitudes of British secondary school pupils to praise, rewards, punishments and reprimands: a further study. *New Zealand Journal of Educational Studies*, 23, 223–34.

Houghton, S., Wheldall, K., Jukes, R. and Sharpe, P. (1988). Are reprimands really necessary? The effects of limited private reprimands and increased private praise on classroom behaviour in four British secondary school classes. Submitted for publication (Centre for Child Study, University of Birmingham).

Houghton, S., Wheldall, K. and Merrett, F. (1988). Classroom behaviour problems which secondary school teachers say they find most troublesome. *British Educational Research Journal*, 14, 295–310.

Huxley, A. (1964). *Essays of a Humanist*. New York: Harper and Row.

Jerram, H., Glynn, T. and Tuck, B. (1988). Responding to the message: providing a social context for children learning to write. *Educational Psychology*, 8, 31–40.

Kiernan, C. (1984). The behavioural approach to language development. In J. Muller (ed.), *Remediating Children's Language: behavioural and naturalistic approaches*. London: Croom Helm.

Knott, T. and Moore, D. W. (1988). The effects of an introductory provision of context on the oral reading behaviour of an above average reader. *Educational Psychology*, 8, 123–6.

Krantz, P. J. and Risley, T. R. (1977). Behavioral ecology in the classroom. In K. D. O'Leary and S. J. O'Leary (eds), *Classroom Management: the successful use of behavior modification*. (2nd edn). New York: Pergamon.

Limbrick, E., McNaughton, S. S. and Glynn, T. (1985). Reading gains for underachieving tutors and tutees in a cross-age tutoring programme. *Journal of Child Psychology and Psychiatry*, 26, 939–53.

Lovaas, O. I. (1977). *The Autistic Child: language development through behaviour modification*. New York: Irvington.

McCracken, R. A. and McCracken, M. J. (1972). *Reading is Only the Tiger's Tail*. San Rafael, Ca.: Leswing Press.

McCracken, R. A. and McCracken, M. J. (1978). Modelling is the key to sustained silent reading. *The Reading Teacher*, 31, 406–8.

McNaughton, S. S. (1978). 'Instructor Attention to Oral Reading Errors: a functional analysis'. Unpublished doctoral thesis, University of Auckland.

McNaughton, S. S. (1981). Low-progress readers and teacher instructional behaviour during oral reading: the risk of maintaining instructional dependence. *The Exceptional Child*, 28, 167–76.

McNaughton, S. S. (1987). *Being Skilled: socialisation of learning to read*. London: Methuen.

McNaughton, S. S. (1988). A history of errors in the analysis of oral reading behaviour. *Educational Psychology*, 8, 21–30.

McNaughton, S. S. and Glynn, T. (1981). Delayed versus immediate attention to oral reading errors. *Educational Psychology*, 1, 57–65.

McNaughton, S. S., Glynn, T. and Robinson, V. (1981). *Parents as Remedial Tutors: issues for home and school*. Wellington: NZCER.

McNaughton, S. S., Glynn, T. and Robinson, V. (1987). *Pause, Prompt and Praise: effective tutoring for remedial reading.* Birmingham: Positive Products.

Madsen, C. H., Jr., Becker, W. C. and Thomas, D. R. (1968). Rules, praise and ignoring: elements of elementary classroom control. *Journal of Applied Behavior Analysis*, 1, 139–50.

Maloney, K. B. and Hopkins, B. L. (1973). The modification of sentence structure and its relationship to subjective judgement of creativity in writing. *Journal of Applied Behavior Analysis*, 6, 425–34.

Marholin, D. I. and Steinman, W. M. (1977). Stimulus control in the classroom as a function of the behaviour reinforced. *Journal of Applied Behavior Analysis*, 10, 465–78.

Medcalf, J. and Glynn, T. (1987). Assisting teachers to implement peer-tutored remedial reading using Pause, Prompt and Praise procedures. *Queensland Guidance Officers Association Journal*, 1, 11–23.

Merrett, F. E. (1981). Studies in behaviour modification in British educational settings. *Educational Psychology*, 1, 13–38.

Merrett, F. and Wheldall, K. (1978). Playing the game: a behavioural approach to classroom management. *Educational Review*, 30, 391–400.

Merrett, F. E. and Wheldall, K. (1982). Does teaching student teachers about behaviour modification techniques improve their teaching performance in the classroom? *Journal of Education for Teaching*, 8, 67–75.

Merrett, F. and Wheldall, K. (1984). Classroom behaviour problems which Junior school teachers find most troublesome. *Educational Studies*, 10, 87–92.

Merrett, F. and Wheldall, K. (1986). Observing Pupils and Teachers In Classrooms (OPTIC): a behavioural observation schedule for use in schools. *Educational Psychology*, 6, 57–70.

Merrett, F. and Wheldall, K. (1987a). Natural rates of teacher approval and disapproval in British primary and middle school classrooms. *British Journal of Educational Psychology*, 57, 95–103.

Merrett, F. E. and Wheldall, K. (1987b). Troublesome classroom behaviours. In N. Hastings and J. Schwieso (eds), *New Directions in Educational Psychology, Vol. II: Behaviour and Motivation.* London: The Falmer Press.

Merrett, F. and Wheldall, K. (1988a). Case studies in Positive Teaching II: more examples showing behavioural strategies in action at the secondary level. *Behavioural Approaches with*

Children, 12, 25–35.

Merrett, F. and Wheldall, K. (1988b) *The Behavioural Approach to Teaching with Secondary Aged Children (BATSAC) Training Package*. Birmingham: Positive Products.

Merrett, F. and Wheldall, K. (1989). Does training of teachers in behavioural methods result in higher pupil productivity? *Educational and Child Psychology* (in press).

Merrett, F., Wilkins, J., Houghton, S. and Wheldall, K. (1988). Rules, sanctions and rewards in secondary schools. *Educational Studies*, 14, 139–49.

Moerk, E. L. (1974). Changes in verbal child–mother interactions with increasing language skills of the child. *Journal of Psycholinguistic Research*, 3, 109–116.

Moore, D. W. and Glynn, T. (1984). Variation in question rate as a function of position in the classroom. *Educational psychology*, 4 233–48.

Morgan, R. and Lyon, E. (1979). 'Paired Reading': a preliminary report on a technique for parental tuition of reading retarded children. *Journal of Child Psychology*, 20, 151–60.

Nafpaktitis, M., Mayer, G. R. and Butterworth, T. (1985). Natural rates of teacher approval and disapproval and their relation to student behaviour in intermediate school classrooms. *Journal of Educational Psychology*, 77, 363–7.

Neale, M. D. (1966). *Neale Analysis of Reading Ability*. London: Macmillan.

O'Connor, G., Glynn, T. and Tuck, B. (1987). Contexts for remedial reading: Practice Reading and Pause, Prompt and Praise tutoring. *Educational Psychology*, 7, 207–23.

O'Rourke, M. and Glynn, T. (1978). Play equipment and adult participation: effects on children's behaviour. In T. Glynn and S. McNaughton (eds), *Behaviour Analysis in New Zealand*. Auckland: New Zealand Council for Educational Research.

Perdue, J. P. and Connor, J. M. (1978). Patterns of touching between pre-school children and male and female teachers. *Child Development*, 49, 1258–62.

Pickthorne, B. and Wheldall, K. (1982). A behavioural approach to teaching subsidiary physics to engineering students. *Educational Psychology*, 2, 193–200.

Pluck, M., Ghafari, E., Glynn, T. and McNaughton, S. (1984). Teacher and parent modelling of recreational reading. *New Zealand Journal of Educational Studies*, 19, 114–23.

Pratt, D. J. (1973). The relationship between type of teacher nonverbal communication and first and second grade reading achievement. *Dissertation Abstracts International*, 34, 6271A.

Risley, T. R. (1977). The ecology of applied behavior analysis. In A. K. Rogers-Warren and S. F. Rogers-Warren (eds), *Ecological Perspectives in Behavior Analysis*. Baltimore: University Park Press.

Russell, A. and Lin, L. G. (1977). Teacher attention and classroom behaviour. *The Exceptional Child*, 24, 148–55.

Rutter, M., Maughan, B., Mortimore, P. and Ouston, J. (1979). *Fifteen Thousand Hours: secondary schools and their effects on children*. London: Open Books.

Scriven, J. and Glynn, T. (1983). Performance feedback on written tasks for low-achieving secondary students. *New Zealand Journal of Educational Studies*, 18, 134–45.

Sharpe, P. (1986). Behaviour modification in the secondary school: a survey of students' attitudes to rewards and praise. *Behavioural Approaches with Children*, 9, 109–12.

Sharpe, P., Wheldall, K., and Merrett, F. (1987). The attitudes of British secondary pupils to praise and reward. *Educational Studies*, 13, 293–302.

Shute, B. and Wheldall, K. (1989). Pitch alterations in British motherese: some preliminary accoustic data. *Journal of Child Language* (in press).

Singh, N. N. and Singh, J. (1984). Antecedent control of oral reading errors and self-corrections by mentally retarded children. *Journal of Applied Behavior Analysis*, 17, 111–19.

Skinner, B. F. (1948). *Walden Two*. New York: Macmillan.

Skinner, B. F. (1957). *Verbal Behavior*. New York: Appleton-Century Crofts.

Skinner, B. F. (1971). *Beyond Freedom and Dignity*. London: Jonathan Cape.

Smith, F. (1978). *Understanding Reading: a psycholinguistic analysis of reading and learning to read* (2nd edn) New York: Holt, Rinehart and Winston.

Smith, H. A. (1979). Nonverbal communication in teaching. *Review of Educational Research*, 49, 631–72.

Snow, C. E. (1977). The development of conversation between mothers and babies. *Journal of Child Language*, 4, 1–22.

Snow, C. E. and Ferguson, C. A. (1977). *Talking to Children: language input and acquisition*. Cambridge: Cambridge University Press.

Thomas, D. R., Becker, W. C. and Armstrong, M. (1968). Production and elimination of disruptive classroom behavior by systematically varying teacher's behaviour. *Journal of Applied Behavior Analysis*, 1, 35–45.

Thomas, J. D., Presland, I. V., Grant, D. and Glynn, T. (1978). Natural rates of teacher approval and disapproval in Grade 7 and Grade 8 classrooms. *Journal of Applied Behavior Analysis*, 11, 91–4.

Topping, K. (1987). Peer tutored paired reading: outcome data from ten projects. *Educational Psychology*, 7, 133–45.

Topping, K. (1988). *The Peer Tutoring Handbook: promoting co-operative learning*. London: Croom Helm.

Vargas, J. (1977). *Behavioural Psychology for Teachers*. New York: Harper and Row.

Vargas, J. (1978). A behavioural approach to the teaching of composition. *Behavior Analyst*, Spring, 16–24.

Wahler, R. G. and Fox, J. J. (1981). Setting events in applied behavior analysis: toward a conceptual and methodological expansion. *Journal of Applied Behavior Analysis*, 14, 327–38.

Wallace, I. and Pear, M. (1977). Self control techniques of famous novelists. *Journal of Applied Behavior Analysis*, 10, 515–25.

Watson, J. B. (1913). Psychology as the behaviorist views it. *Psychological Review*, 20, 158–77.

Watson, J. B. (1928). *The Psychological Care of Infant and Child*. London: Allen and Unwin.

Wells, G. (1984). *Language in the Pre-school Years*. London: Cambridge University Press.

West, C. and Wheldall, K. (1988). Waiting for teacher: the frequency and duration of times children spend waiting for teacher attention in infant school classrooms. *British Educational Research Journal*, 15 (2).

Wheldall, D. and Wheldall, K. (1984). Distar in the day nursery: an experimental evaluation of Distar Language 1. *Educational Review*, 36, 287–301.

Wheldall, K. (1981). A before C or the use of behavioural ecology in classroom management. In P. Gurney (ed.), *Behaviour Modification in Education. Perspectives No. 5*. Exeter: School of Education, University of Exeter. (Also in N. Entwistle (ed.) *New Directions in Educational Psychology, Vol. 1: Learning and Teaching*. London: Falmer Press. 1985).

Wheldall, K. (1982). Behavioural pedagogy or behavioural overkill? *Educational Psychology*, 2, 181–4.

Wheldall, K. and Austin, R. (1980). Successful behaviour modification in the secondary school: a reply to McNamara and Harrop. *Occasional Papers of the Division of Educational and Child Psychology of the British Psychological Society*, 4, 3–9.

Wheldall, K., Bevan, K. and Shortall (1986). A touch of reinforcement: the effects of contingent teacher touch on the classroom behaviour of young children. *Educational Review*, 38, 207–16.

Wheldall, K. and Congreve, S. (1980). The attitudes of British teachers towards behaviour modification. *Educational Review*, 32, 53–65.

Wheldall, K. and Entwistle, J. (1988). Back in the USSR: the effect of teacher modelling of silent reading on pupils' reading behaviour in the primary school classroom. *Educational Psychology*, 8, 51–66.

Wheldall, K. and Glynn, T. (1988). Contingencies in contexts: a behavioural interactionist perspective in education. *Educational Psychology*, 8, 5–19.

Wheldall, K., Houghton, S. and Merrett, F. (1989). Natural rates of teacher approval and disapproval in British secondary school classrooms. *British Journal of Educational Psychology*, 59, 38–48.

Wheldall, K. and Lam, J. (1987). Rows versus tables II: the effects of two classroom seating arrangements on classroom disruption rate, on-task behaviour and teacher behaviour in three special school classes. *Educational Psychology* 8, 303–12.

Wheldall, K. and Merrett, F. (1984). *Positive Teaching: the behavioural approach*. London: Allen and Unwin.

Wheldall, K. and Merrett, F. (1985). *The Behavioural Approach to Teaching Package for use in primary and middle schools (BATPACK)*. Birmingham: Positive Products.

Wheldall, K. and Merrett, F. (1986). Managing troublesome behaviour in primary and secondary classrooms. *Schoolmaster and Career Teacher*, Spring, 27–31.

Wheldall, K. and Merrett, F. (1987a). What is the behavioural approach to teaching? In N. Hastings and J. Schwieso (eds) *New Directions in Educational Psychology, Vol. II: Behaviour and Motivation*. London: The Falmer Press.

Wheldall, K. and Merrett, F. (1987b). Training teachers to use the behavioural approach to classroom management: the development of BATPACK. In K. Wheldall (ed.), *The Behaviourist in the Classroom*. London: Allen and Unwin.

Wheldall, K. and Merrett, F. E. (1988). Which classroom behaviours do primary school teachers say they find most troublesome?

Educational Review, 40, 13–27.

Wheldall, K., Merrett, F. and Borg, M. (1985). The Behavioural Approach to Teaching Package (BATPACK): an experimental evaluation. *British Journal of Educational Psychology*, 55, 65–75.

Wheldall, K., Merrett, F., Worsley, M., Colmar, S. and Parry, R. (1986). Evaluating effectiveness: a case study evaluation of the Behavioural Approach to Teaching Package (BATPACK). *Educational and Child Psychology*, 3, 33–44.

Wheldall, K. and Mettem, P. (1985). Behavioural peer tutoring: training 16-year-old tutors to employ the 'pause, prompt and praise' method with 12-year-old remedial readers. *Educational Psychology*, 5, 27–44.

Wheldall, K., Morris, M., Vaughan, P. and Ng, Y. Y. (1981). Rows versus tables: an example of the use of behavioural ecology in two classes of eleven year old children. *Educational Psychology*, 1, 171–184.

Wheldall, K. and Olds, D. (1987). Of sex and seating: the effects of mixed and same-sex seating arrangements in junior classrooms. *New Zealand Journal of Educational Studies*, 22, 71–85.

Wheldall, K., Wenban-Smith, J., Morgan, A. and Quance, B. (1988). Reading: how do teachers typically tutor? Submitted for publication (Centre for Child Study, University of Birmingham).

Wheldall, K. and Wheldall, D. (1981). School meals, praise and contingent dessert: an attempt to improve eating behaviour in the nursery classroom. *Behavioural Approaches with Children*, 5(2), 30–46.

Wheldall, K. Wheldall, D. and Winter, S. (1983). *Seven Supertactics for Superparents*. Windsor: NFER/Nelson. Republished Birmingham: Positive Products, 1986.

White, M. A. (1975). Natural rates of teacher approval and disapproval in the classroom. *Journal of Applied Behavior Analysis*, 8, 91–4.

Whitehead, F., Capey, A., Maddren, W. and Wellings, A. (1977). *Children and their Books*. London: Macmillan.

Wilson, M. G. and Glynn, T. (1983). Increasing self-selection and self-location of words by mildly retarded children during story writing. *The Exceptional Child*, 30, 210–20.

Wong, P. and McNaughton, S. (1980). The effects of prior provision of context on the oral reading proficiency of a low progress reader. *New Zealand Journal of Educational Studies*, 15, 169–75.

Index

Index by Frank Merrett